Welcome to Mintland

D1418063

Eric J Moran

ISBN:1517536596
ISBN-13:978-1517536596

DEDICATION

This book is dedicated to my daughters and to the 2014-2015 Minnie Mints and Mickey. Your effort, teamwork and belief in yourself helped you achieve a lifelong memory that will never be taken away. May you cherish this moment forever and reflect upon this as you go through life. May your path be filled with full outs that hit, tumbles that never bust and stunts that never fall. If you do not know what I am talking about and are about to read this book, Let me help... 5,6,7,8!!!!

CONTENTS

Acknowledgments

1   The Beginning of Something Special

2   Tryouts and a Few Unusual Additions

3   Introducing the Stunt of Death

4   The March to Jams

5   The First Competition: Encore

6   WSF Louisville Kentucky

7   Athletic Championships and Little Cheersport

8   Preparing for the Big 3

9   NCA

10   The Peppermint Plot Twist

11   UCA

12   The Road to Summit

ACKNOWLEDGMENTS

My Dear Daughters,

I wrote this story for you both, but when I began it I had not realized that girls grow quicker than books. As a result you have already moved on to the next phase in your lives, and by the time this is printed and published you will be older still. But some day you will be on a team or in a situation in life where I hope you reference this book. You can then take it down from a cluttered shelf or box, dust it off, and remember this time in our lives. As you get older, lives get complicated and relationships challenged. I will probably be too old to understand and will not get it, but I shall still be your affectionate Daddy and I watched you do the impossible with your teammates. This book will forever be a reminder of your passion for life, allstar cheer and the limitless talent that you have in whatever you set out to do.

Daddy

.

1 THE BEGINNING OF SOMETHING SPECIAL

As the 2013-2014 season wrapped up for the Stingray Allstars it was quite evident that next year would be a very different year. With their first year in the books at one of the most world renowned gyms in the world, my young daughters found a passion for something they truly love. As a father, I was captivated as well. Two very close sisters spent every waking hour creating new routines, tumbling in grocery stores and stunting on the back of couches. I could not help but get caught up in their enthusiasm. It was more than that for me. I fed off my daughters' enthusiasm, and learning about all-star cheer became a passion of mine. I became a student and a sponge. After all, when you have a four year old and you take her to The Champions League movie and she critiques every Level 5 team on form and being clean you better know your stuff.

The Stingray Allstars Peppermint are comprised of six, seven and eight year olds. They are a group of kids that live within a 30 mile radius of the Stingrays gym in Marietta, Ga (a few come from farther). Level 1 means they are restricted by what skills they can throw in a routine. Basically, their hands or feet can never leave the floor for any tumbling. Stunts are comprised of limited height and multiple bases to support the athlete as to limit exposure to injury. Fun to watch, but compared to a Senior Level 5 team it typically does not draw the same level of crowds or fanfare.

It was time for The Summit and Worlds competitions in Orlando, Florida. Friends and teammates gathered at our house for viewing parties to watch our beloved gym take on some of the most gifted athletes in the World. Our Senior Level 5 team, The Stingray Allstars Orange were about

1

to take the stage for the final time. They had an opportunity to win their 8th World Championship in which they succeeded in doing. It was a special time for our gym as Orange is a staple for Stingrays. Everyone looks up to them and models them. Although Orange did not dominate every competition like in years past, they pulled it out when it counted most and when almost everyone counted them out. The World title gave my daughters a confidence of belonging and pride as they both practiced next to Orange and watched their every move at least twice a week.

The new season was coming up quickly and we knew my youngest child would be on a tiny team. The "Grape Rays" as they are called are adored by many across the nation. This team is comprised of four year olds and five year olds. What the coaches do with these little athletes is absolutely amazing. People seek out and watch as the Grape Rays boggle minds in every competition perfecting routines and building believers on what these kids can do together as teammates.

My older daughter was working to get on a Mini Level 2 team. She was working extremely hard to perfect required tumbling skills to meet Level 2 requirements. Tryouts were coming up and she knew she had to put in the hours. It was going to be close, but I think we knew she may come up a bit short executing the Level 2 skills this year.

At Stingrays there is unintentional pressure applied to go to the next level. Friendships and bonds built from previous teams help drive these athletes to stay with each other for more reasons than one. The bonds that are created over a season are indescribable. You want to stay on the team with your friends. Unfortunately, skill levels change and the speed of which athletes pick up tumbling stunting and body positions skills varies for multiple reasons. Growth spurts, athleticism, talent and work ethic, maturity all factor in when building desired skill levels. At Stingrays they build teams to win, period. They very carefully analyze the athletes to build a perfect formula for success, from the most prestigious Level 5 teams all the way down to the Tiny Level.

While All Star cheerleading is defined by the incredible athleticism of the Level 5 All Star Cheerleaders, this story is about a special group of Level 1 All Star Cheerleaders that inspired many. Level 5 cheerleaders are incredible athletes who sacrifice everything to perfect a two minute and thirty second routine. They compete against teams around the world perfecting tumbling, stunting and dance. The competitions bring tens of thousands of viewers and create rabid fans from all over the world that follow their teams religiously at competitions, on ESPN and CBS Sports. There is serious sacrifice, dedication, hard practices and risk of serious injury all to be the best in the world.

The last month of the cheer season entails working four to five times a week in the gym perfecting your tumbling and stunting skills in preparation for tryouts. Kids work their tails off to try and get to the next level team. As a dad, it was important to me to make sure my daughter was set up to succeed, not so much that she moved to the next level. The coaching staff for the entire gym is incredible. While many coaches have their strengths and weaknesses the entire staff compliments each other perfectly to make sure they maximize each athlete's talents.

My daughter was on Peppermint in her first year which was a very successful season. Peppermint won every single competition they entered except the first one where they finished in 5th place. The coaching staff was incredible. If I had my way, I would want my daughter to be on the team again to build her fundamentals and build her confidence for the years ahead. She had her sights set on staying with her friends from the previous season. We would soon find out if she could achieve that dream or not.

While the previous season at Stingrays was successful, it did not feel that the entire gym was happy with the overall performance of all the teams. No one said it directly, but it was felt. As a parent that spent four to five days a week in the gym, I could tell the intensity level was ramping up going into the new 2014-2015 tryouts season. There was a new energy, it was going to be different for all levels you could just feel it.

Eric J. Moran

2 TRYOUTS AND A FEW UNUSUAL ADDITIONS

As tryouts loomed ahead, athletes were cramming in extra tumbling classes to perfect the pass they had to perform at tryouts. Many of the kids would work for hours in hopes of making their dream team for that season. It was May and tryouts fever was in the air.

As the tryout day inched closer, we learned the gym was going to do something different this year. In years past, Stingrays would post the results from tryouts on their website. This year the gym wanted to try something a little more personal. After the coaches labored to align the talent with the appropriate teams the coaches were going to call each athlete personally to tell them which team they were on. It was a nice touch and I was looking forward to my daughters getting their call.

Tryouts end on the weekend and it takes the coaches a few days to iron out their teams. The coaches literally lock themselves in the gym for about forty eight hours to figure out where all the hundreds of athletes are going to be placed. It is a long and grueling process for them. On the other hand, it is a long and grueling process for the parents and athletes as well. The anticipation of what team you are going to be on is captivating. Athletes and parents light up Twitter with speculation of which team they are going to be on. It is truly a fun and humorous time as you are literally waiting for all the coaches to finalize the teams and make the calls.

Over the course of the first year I had built up a fun following on Twitter. I loved sharing the special moments of my daughters' teams over the course of the year. It was intoxicating to share all of the funny things the kids did and said. It was important for me to document. It was a time in my life where I felt compelled to not only live in the moment but try my best to document it.

At first, it was just for my personal enjoyment. I loved being able to re-live funny moments that I would normally take for granted later in life. I wanted my kids to be able to look back on this time and enjoy it as much as I did. While doing all of this, many people loved the snap shot into the life of a tiny and mini all-star cheerleader. It helped me bond with parents who so related with the experiences their older kids put them through while they were young and in cheer. Honestly, I think it was refreshing to see the innocence and passion these kids shared on a daily basis.

Creating this twitter following also allowed me an opportunity to meet people I would not normally meet from other teams. In all-star cheer there is an undeniable comradery between both athletes and parents. The sacrifices made by both are truly amazing. In order for a gym the size of Stingrays to survive there has to be a support mechanism from everyone. Complete strangers would come up to me and say "I love when you share the funny and successful moments from your children's teams. I am so glad you enjoy the time in this sport because it will go so fast."

It was almost tryout announcement time and all the athletes and parents congregated on twitter waiting to see if the coaches selected their teams. The coaches began sending out taunting tweets to let us know the end was near. As you may know, most athletes and parents of athletes are very "Type A" personality; the tweets were only stirring the angst of wanting to know what team you are on. The coaches knew it, and to me it was hilarious, to others it was agonizing. As the night went on, we received more hints via twitter that the teams were close to being done. An email was sent out from the gym letting us know that the coaches would be calling us at 6pm the following day to notify athletes. We were all very excited.

My wife and I knew which team our youngest was going to be on, there was no suspense there. She had just turned 5 years old and age limitations prevented her from moving up to another team. We had a hunch with my oldest daughter that she may stay on the team she was on last year. She was close to having the skills needed, but at Stingrays you need to have the skills "mastered" before you will be considered.

As the phone rang, the first call came for my youngest daughter. She had received word that she would be on the "Grape Rays" for a second year. She was excited and we made a big deal out of it for her. Little did she know that she did not have a choice.

Ten minutes later the phone rang for my second daughter. My wife was upstairs getting the kids organized for the following day and I was downstairs in the office working. I was waiting for the response from my oldest. I was expecting her to come flying downstairs to tell me which team she was on. The moment was taking longer than I had anticipated. I heard footsteps coming through the kitchen and voices. The phone was on speaker and my wife was speaking to the coaches. My wife walked into the office and handed the phone to me. I looked up and gave her a puzzled look. She said the coach wants to speak with you.

I took the phone a little perplexed. The conversation went like this. "Uh hello" "Hey Eric, its Coach Ashley." "I wanted to let you know that we have selected Kaitlyn to be on Peppermint this year." Me: "Aww that is awesome I am excited for her" Coach Ashley: "The reason I am talking to you is I was wondering if you would mind changing your twitter handle from @cRayCheerDad to @cRayMintTeamDad?" Me: "Um sure, but why? Ashley: "Well I guess what I am asking is would you be our team rep for Peppermint this year?"

I was floored. Honestly, I did not know what to say. Traditionally, this role has not been filled by Dads. My daughter was looking at me with desperate anticipation of me accepting the offer. How could I refuse? It was truly an honor to be asked and I graciously accepted. My wife thought I was nuts, we had a full plate already how were we going to navigate the added responsibility. I told her we would figure it out, we always do. I told Coach Ashley I would be honored to do it.

At that point my mind started racing. Kaitlyn was so excited and I did not want to let her down. In my mind, I was excited too. Although I had no idea what I was about to get myself into. I knew we had incredible Team Mom's the previous year that helped us stay organized and on top of things. I was not sure I would be able to live up to what they did, but I would give it a shot. I started to think of all the cool things the teams did together the previous year. I was not sure I could pull it off, but at that moment I wanted to make a point to focus on the kids and the kids only. Stuff and parties were nice. Experiences last a lifetime. That would be my motto for the entire season and my goal was to adhere to it.

The first week of practices started and it was exciting for the kids. When you meet your team for the first time it is fun, but awkward at the same time. You have a few friends from last year, but many have moved on to other teams or aged out. It's a new year, with a new nucleus. The exciting part is meeting all new kids and building new friendships. When the team assembled on the mats everyone noticed something different with the team. There was a boy on the team this year!

Many of the older teams have boys on their squad. For the younger teams, it is rare for a boy to be on the team. I was excited for the group. Part of this journey is expanding your horizons and working together as a team. Embracing diversity is paramount in cheer. In all levels you will meet every race, creed, and color. The life lesson here is that you will need to learn to work with everyone, not just the people who you have traditionally become comfortable with. Beecher was a kid that absolutely loved being part of this team from the get go. The rest of the team embraced him after a few practices and he quickly was part of the Peppermint family. It is easy to shun someone on a team if they are not like you. This team was special; this team embraced everyone and everything. It was impressive to watch up close. The confidence building in each other early in the season would help them grow later on in the season; we just did not know how far it would take them. After embracing a boy, little did the team know they were soon going to experience a similar feeling when they met their "Team Mom".

After a few practices, I began gathering parent contact information. One of the many duties of a "Team Rep" is disseminating information out to the parents from the coaches. One day at practice the kids were gathering by the parents and one of the Peppermints or "Mints" asked what time practice was on Thursdays. One of the parents said I am sure the "Team Rep" will let us know. I could see where this conversation was headed. I had dreaded facing it, but here it was staring me right in the face.

The next statement out of her mouth was "Well who is our Team Mom cause I need to know?" I gently saddled up to her and said "I am your Team Mom and practices will start at 6pm." She looked at me in complete horror and said "Well you're not a Mom you are a Dad!" We all laughed hysterically and luckily the little Mint warmed up to me quickly. I was worried the team would feel awkward with me representing them, but after a while they all embraced me with open arms and I did the same with them. It was the start of a very special relationship.

Eric J. Moran

3 INTRODUCING THE STUNT OF DEATH

As the season began coaches started placing the athletes in the routine. Early in the season there is quite a bit of experimentation to find out what the team is capable of. Watching the team early on it was evident Coach Ashley had big aspirations for this team. As the practices went on you could tell this team was extremely talented across the board. As I say this, please keep in mind I understand this is a Level 1 All Star Cheer team. Watching the team as a novice observer, I noticed they were extremely clean and fundamentally sound in technique which is extremely difficult to do across the board on any level team including Level 5.

As June 2014 approached it was almost time for Stunt Camp. This a time where the team carves out a designated extended practice to work on the stunt section of the routine. The team will practice for extended hours and do nothing but assemble their stunt sequence for the year. It is a big week for a team. It is where the heart of the routine develops and it is a great bonding exercise for the team and coaches. The camp is closed off to parents and spectators. Many of the Stingray coaches will help other teams and give advice on what the stunts should look like and "ideate" what the team is capable of.

The first day of stunt camp came and my daughter was excited. Kaitlyn was a base and back spot, this camp is a fun time for bases and back spots as they will be able to try new stunts and get acquainted with their new flyers for the season. As the experimentation began, it was exciting to see what the team was trying to execute. Coach Ashley was clearly pushing this team this year. At first glance, I thought what they were trying was a bit ambitious, but I liked the aggressiveness and confidence she showed in this team. At first, they attempted a pendulum stunt where the flyer is basically used as a jump rope for lack of a better term. After a few attempts, it was apparent that the bases were not tall enough to make the pendulum work for this year.

After about an hour, something started to take shape. Being the Team Dad, I was one of the only parents allowed in the viewing area. I had another Mom with me to help with getting the kids organized and food together for lunch and snack. She was helping me get the snack and lunches together. I stopped and said "Holy Moly Marilyn watch this!" We both watched as the team put together stunt that was pretty impressive. We could not hear what was happening down on the floor but you could tell the team and the coaches were pretty excited. At this point in the season, you could tell when this group got excited. They all started jumping up and down like popcorn. After a few more tries with a couple of the other groups, the stunt camp concluded and the team had created what would be their signature stunt that set the pace for the year.

As parents came to pick up their children they were curious to find out how the Mints did and wanted to know what they were working on. My response was "If they can perfect this stunt they are going to do amazing things this year." Being the curious group that they are, they wanted me to explain the stunt to them. After thinking about it all I could say was, "You just have to see it; I cannot do the stunt justice by explaining it". Unfortunately, that was not a very popular answer as all the parents were excited to see what the team had come up with.

Practices started up again as normal and the team began to work on the routine and stunt sequence. As the team started to form the stunt, I looked over to a few of the parents and said, "Ok, here we go watch this." As the parents focused in on what the team was doing, instantaneously about five Moms let out a collective gasp all at once! Oh my goodness! They are going to do that in the routine? I responded "yup" as the practice went on the stunt groups were trying to get their timing and technique coordinated in perfecting this ambitious stunt.

As a parent, early Peppermint practices were difficult to watch, especially for the parents of flyers. The stunt involved a lot of faith in each other as a base and flyer. Trust in each other and technique would define this team as the season went on and it started with this stunt. The flyer was lifted into the air about four feet off the ground with two bases holding each of their feet. Once the flyer was set, the back spot violently yanked the flyers feet straight back as hard as they could and the bases would then form a basket and catch her while she was careening face first toward the floor. For a group of six, seven and eight year olds this was a very challenging stunt. The coaching had to be flawless, the technique impeccable, and the faith and trust in each other rock solid.

The team continued to practice and early on it was far from perfect. There is no easy way to describe some of the stunt falls. When the stunt did not go right, the flyer literally went face first into the spring floor as her arms extended out to form a bird flying through the air. There were many gasps when things did not go right. It was uncomfortable to watch but impressive all at the same time. Each time the stunt failed the flyer would bounce back up off the floor (sometimes after a few tears) and jump back into practicing the stunt. After a few weeks the parents had a new name for the stunt sequence "The Stunt of Death".

Breaking from Stunt Camp

4 THE MARCH TO JAMS

Practices continued and the team pieced together their routine. It was coming together. Peppermint started the year as a Large Mini team. With so many kids that need to work together as a team the athletes needed to bond. The parents felt that a little team building exercise would be a great start to the season. We organized a simple potluck picnic outing at a local park so the kids could get together and blow off some steam and have fun. On the surface it sounded like a great idea. We had lunch after practice together as a team. Had a few treats, and played a few games. It was interesting to watch the kids play games. They instantly started cheering for each other, not against each other. In the hula hoop contest once someone was out, they immediately began cheering for the others still in the game. It was not earth shattering, but it was something that struck me as unique. That small bit of kindness would blossom in the future. The parents began to chat amongst themselves to get more familiar with each other. It started out as a great time for all to get to know one another.

One thing you need to know about a group of Stingrays, you will not be able to leave them unattended for any period of time. If you are not attentive, you will have to deal with them potentially giving you a heart attack. Every two to three minutes we would have to stop the kids from building huge pyramids in gravel, tumbling on the cement, building stunt sequences off the side of garbage cans, you know, the normal stuff cheerleaders do in their free time. After about fifteen minutes of this, the parents thought it might be a good idea to move the kids from the picnic area over to the park and slides so they could blow off some more steam. I concurred that was a fabulous idea!

As we moved the team over to the park area a few team members darted toward the slides and monkey bars. That lasted all of about five minutes. The team went back to what they know best, to have fun cheering. They began to create their own mini routines and stunt for fun. The team was having a blast and working together. The parents were all chatting amongst themselves. After about fifteen minutes there was a small commotion going on where the team was playing. It seemed a few young boys who were at the park saying something to the Peppermints. We could not make out what was being said, but you could tell it was competitive in nature. As the discussion grew in intensity you could see more of the group getting involved. It seemed the boys were challenging the Peppermints.

One thing you need to know about cheerleaders, no matter what the age, no matter what the circumstance they will naturally stick together and defend when faced with adversity. A few of the Peppermints who were still playing on the swings ran over to see what the commotion was. Next thing you know we have about fourteen Peppermints standing together making sure nothing happened to their teammates. It was happening, without knowing, they had each other's back almost instinctively. Peppermint began to form stunt groups and they were going to show the boys what they could do. The stunt group put Carter up in a "Teddy Bear" and they started to tumble to the routine they were assembling. As a few of the parents started to stroll over to make sure the confrontation did not get ugly. The two boys stated, "Wow that is not bad" but can you do this?" The boy who could not have been more than seven or eight years old started running and threw a round off triple back handspring with a layout over the other little boy.

The parents stood and watched in amazement watching the entire thing. It was impressive to watch the Peppermints bond together and make sure they had each other's back. It was also cool to see the team congratulate the little boy and tell him that his tumbling was awesome. They ended up having a mutual respect for each other which was refreshing to see. As a parent, the most important thing for me was to watch the team support the little boy. This respect the Mints showed the young man would help define their success and would also show up in the Stingrays gym in a big way as they supported the other Stingray teams throughout the year. This was the birth of the squad we would know as the Minnie Mints and Mickey for the rest of the year. Twenty one girls and of course Beecher who posed as Mickey. The team was bonding together and it would only get better from here.

One of the most anticipated time of the year is when the teams receive their music. In All Star Cheer, the music your team receives will forever define your season, it is an anthem. For parents, it is a love/hate relationship. It means a two minute and thirty second song on endless repeat for about seven months of the year. The coaches help assemble the music and it is synchronized via count sheets to the routine. The first few times I listened to the music, I noticed a part of the music that seemed interesting to me. In the first thirty seconds of the music there were five sequential "snaps" or "popping" sound effects to the music. I listened to it numerous times and then I put two and two together and figured it out. Coach Ashley was going to set "Stunt of Death" to music. It was genius!

That night at practice, sure enough Peppermint started to piece it together and practice it. At first it was not pretty. It took a lot to get everyone positioned properly and the music was fast. There was no margin for error. After many attempts it started to come together. There were many falls and stumbles, but that is to be expected.

Over the course of a few weeks unfortunately we lost a few Peppermints for various reasons. This took our team from twenty two Mints down to eighteen. Losing a few team members is unfortunate, but many times it cannot be avoided. With this change the team went from five stunt groups to four. Being the resilient team that they are the Peppermints just kept chugging along to perfect their routine. After a few weeks the rest of the routine was complete. The dance, the pyramid, the stunt sequence and the music all came together for something magical. It was rough, but I could see what Coach Ashley was shooting for and if they could get this routine perfect, they were going to go along way.

Towards the end of summer the excitement started to build as you could see the routine come together. During the stunt of death there were not as many face plants. The technique was getting stronger and the team was building confidence in their ability. Peppermint began to run through the routine and began to go full out as everything started to come together. They were a few months away from "The Jams" which was the Stingrays first full exhibition of the season. They had a long way to go to perfection but the routine was coming together.

The deadline for the Jams helped set the intensity level and created a sense of urgency to work together as a team. Peppermint wanted to be perfect for The Jams. To say that this group of Mini's was competitive would be putting it lightly. Peppermint wanted to steal the show in everything they did. It was fun to watch as a parent. You could see the confidence in each other build. They fed off each other and helped each other with every full out.

Unfortunately, the team suffered a setback as one of our star flyers broke her hand in a freak tumbling accident. It was a scary moment for all of us because the break was not a normal break. At that moment, reality sets in and the routine is not important any more. When someone gets hurt like that it becomes very real. She had a spiral fracture in her hand that may have required surgery. As a parent, it scares the life out of you; it is your worst nightmare. No one wants to see a child with a serious injury. Luckily after a few second opinions she was going to be ok. What was more impressive is that the injured Mint never missed a practice. Even with the broken hand she watched intently during each practice and continued to learn with the team. The perseverance and dedication from her was a huge life lesson and it went along way with the team. The team was also very thankful for Lexi who filled in for the mint during the injury.

A few weeks away from The Jams Peppermint began to go full out on a regular basis. The intensity level was ramped up on all the teams in the gym. In the parent viewing area, when full outs start, the parents stop what they are doing huddle to watch the teams as they perform. I will never forget the first time Peppermint went full out in front of a group of parents from other teams. One of the most important traits of Stingrays is that they always support each other. There is always healthy competition, but at the end of the day everyone has each other's back.

As Peppermint assembled to go full out in front of the Senior Medium 5 team "Peach" they all sat down on the side of the mat to watch the incredible "Peach Rays" go full out. To set the stage here, it is typically not normal for a mini team to go full out with a Senior Team. It happens occasionally but is not the norm.

As Peach started to walk out on the mat there was a roaring cheer coming from the mats. So much that many of the parents started walking over in the parents viewing area to see what was going on. You see, normally you will hear a typical polite applause and encouragement when a team went on the mat. This was different, Peppermint practiced alongside Peach for the better part of the summer and they admired what they were working on. Peach was working on their own magical routine and both of the teams knew it. While both teams practiced, through it all, there were smiles that lit up the gym on both teams. Peppermint had a respect for Peach and it was showing through.

As Peach began the routine it was extremely impressive. The Senior Level 5 team gracefully flew through the air with flawless stunts and impeccable tumbling. The parent viewing area was electric as clearly there was something special going on with Peach as well. Towards the second half of the routine, all of a sudden everyone heard a resounding yell from a group on the mat. "I GOT 99 PROBLEMS BUT A PEACH AINT ONE!" we look down and sure enough it was Peppermint screaming one of the voice overs from the Peach music. It was impressive because the music for Peach had only been out for a few days the Mints listened to it and latched onto it from the start. Peach was already hitting their routine, after Peppermint began screaming for them, they kicked it up another notch as Peach started into the dance sequence they were working on and entire gym was ignited. Peach hit, and the Mints were ecstatic for them. As Peach left the mat you could tell a special bond had just formed. Many of girls on Peach gave a few hugs to the Mints as they headed on the mat to follow up what Peach just did. It was not normal to see two teams bond with the age gap that existed. It was really special to witness. The relationship between the two teams would blossom as the year went on.

As Peppermint took the mats they were beaming with confidence as they wanted to show all the big kids that they could do just as well. As the music blared, the team started with their opening, so far so good, everyone hit their tumbling and things were going well. As they started into the next sequence everyone held their breath. It was coming. The team put the flyers up perfectly and then a large collective gasp erupted coupled with a few OH MY GAWDS!

It was the first time the Peach parents saw the "Stunt of Death" set to music. It worked, and oh man did it work! The rest of the routine went extremely well. There were a few things to clean up but overall it looked incredible. That was exciting in itself. What was even more exciting was the buzz from the routine after they were done. All of the parents were blown away by the Peppermint routine. The team was bouncing with pride as all the hard work from the spring and summer was starting to pay off.

What was even more exciting to them is that the Peach Rays were so excited for them as well. The parents could not stop talking about the routine or the "Stunt of Death". The Stunt takes unsuspecting viewers by surprise. As fans of All Star cheer as an observer of routines you are trained to look for sudden falls and quick movements. To the trained eye, once you see someone fall quickly, it normally means a stunt fall, bobble or a deduction. What made the "Stunt of Death" so special is that it caught everyone by surprise. At first glance, it looked like everyone was falling, but once the stunt was over you realized it was choreographed and was aligned perfectly with the music. Out of pure coincidence Peach had a similar signature stunt, it was only fitting that both teams shared the unique identity.

With the Jams coming closer the intensity level of practices increased. The number of full outs leveled up, along with the expectations of the team. The routine looked very sharp, and the confidence was increasing within the group. The "Minnie Mints and Mickey" as they were called were really starting to come together. The talk around the gym was very flattering. Many of the parents outside of Peppermint noticed how well the team was executing their routine this early in the year. What was even more exciting to see is that the team was really coming together as friends.

The week of Jams was upon us and the electricity was in the air. The last week of practice entailed numerous full outs and full out parties. The Jams is an exhibition, but it serves multiple purposes to Stingrays. It is a way to ramp up the intensity level for the new team members to simulate the pressures of the competition season. It is a great dry run for each of the teams to see how they will react to the larger audience and to the spotlight.

It was a long summer and it was exciting to see the teams finally hit the floor. As Peppermints performance time inched closer my heart began to thump. Although my daughter is on the team, being the team dad I internally adopted all the Peppermints. Each one of the kids had a special place in my heart. After watching all the trials and tribulations over the summer, from illness to injury, overcoming challenges within the team and watching individual victories in their tumbling and watching them grow as people, I really wanted them to do well. Coach Ashley gave them a big challenge in this routine and they responded. My younger daughter performed on the Grape Rays a few minutes before and they did incredibly well. That helped my nerves a little bit, but not much. As they announced Peppermint was on deck, my palms began to sweat and I began to breathe heavily. My wife noticed I was a bit nervous and chuckled at me. I was eager to find out how the crowd would respond to "Stunt of Death" I wanted Peppermint to hit perfectly as they had in practices.

As Peppermint ran on to the mat they looked extremely confident and ready to go. As the music began they executed the opening perfectly. Next the transition to "Stunt of Death" as each of the flyers were in position for their drop. The first flyer dropped and then the second, third, etc.. The large gasp from the crowd said it all. Many of the parents grabbed their mouths and chuckled as they were taken aback and shocked at how the stunt was executed. The rest of the routine finished into the dance and the Peppermints got a huge round of applause as they finished the routine. They had a few things to work on collectively and I would not call the performance a "hit" but the foundation was there. Now it was time to clean everything up for the start of competition season.

5 THE FIRST COMPETITION ENCORE

The team was excited about their performance at "The Jams". Coach Ashley gave them a lot of encouragement but also told them they could do much better, and they all agreed. The work continued to perfect the routine for the "Encore" competition. Encore was a one day competition that was in Atlanta. The competition was a great way to introduce the electric atmosphere of a competition to the new members of the team who have never experienced a true competition before. If you have never been to an All Star Cheer competition before it can be a very intimidating experience for everyone.

Competitions are organized chaos. Parents, coaches and teams scurry around a huge convention center to make sure every team and child is ready. It takes a complete effort from parents, athletes and coaches to make sure all teams are in synch. The preparation that goes into making sure all athletes are ready to compete is astounding. The uniforms, the makeup, the hair, it is all a coordinated effort to make sure everyone looks uniform and mentally ready. The beautiful thing about the Stingrays program is that they have the routine down pat. From the meet times in the morning, to making sure parents are separated from teams to make sure the athletes get their head in the game. They are a world class program for a reason.

On the ride into the convention center we as a family were getting ready. On the drive to the convention center the conversation normally revolves around nerves and worrying about the competition. On this ride, the discussion was about how Peppermint was going to finish this year. My youngest was extremely confident in the Grapes routine. Kelsie has a confidence about her that is impressive. I attribute that confidence to her incredible coaches. She did not seemed phased at all that her team was about to go on stage in front of thousands of people and compete against 6 other great Tiny teams. I have to keep reminding myself she is only five years old and she has nerves of steel. The conversation focused on the Peppermints. Kaitlyn was getting very nervous. She asked me if I remembered what place Peppermint finished at the Encore competition last year. I did not want to bring it up, but I answered "Yes honey, you guys finished in 5th place last year." This competition was very traumatic for Peppermint last year. Stingrays are a very successful program and a 5th place finish is a very rare occurrence. The team was nervous and was in a different mental state during this competition last year. They went on to have an incredible season, but it got off to a slow start during the previous Encore competition. The girls all remembered that feeling and did not ever want to feel that way again. I told my daughter the only thing I expect from her is to do her very best, and that's all I could ask for. At this young age it is so important for the kids to fall in love with the sport. It should not be stressful for them it should be fun but challenging.

As we walked into the convention center I started to get very nervous. It just hit me; this was my first competition as team Dad. It was hard enough as a family getting two girls ready for competition. We had to do that, and then I had to communicate with eighteen other parents to make sure everyone made it in the building on time and everyone was ready for competition. Multiple texts started pouring in. "Where do we park?" "Where are we meeting?" "I am running late" "I am stuck in traffic" it was very overwhelming. The trick for me personally is trying to stay calm. I am not a multi-tasker at all. So trying to stay calm and composed was my biggest challenge. The second your athletes see you freaking out about something their anxiety level peaks, and their head can get out of the game. The trick is to keep them calm and composed until the coaches take the team to warm ups.

As a parent, all you focus on is making sure your child is ready to leave for warm ups. Then you go find your seat and wait. That's it! Well we got my youngest off to their coaches and the Grapes were off to warm ups. The coaches parade the team down the hall as all the four and five year olds hold hands and walk together as a team. It is a great tradition to watch, as all the parents cheer as they walk down the corridor.

My focus now switched to Peppermints. I was taking a head count and we still were two people short. We still had a few minutes before the scheduled meet time. After a few minutes, all the team members arrived safely. Phew! The first part of my day was complete. As it grew closer to leaving for warm ups, the focus then shifted to no one killing themselves or hurting each other before a competition. You see, this team was very active and with them being six, seven and eight year old kids they had a LOT of energy before competitions. They were all very excited and ready to go. That means uncontrolled spontaneous tumbling, attempts at stunting in the hallway, launching American Girls Dolls in the air and trying to stunt them, all of this at 7:30 in the morning. With each attempted stunt or tumble pass your heart skips a beat because this place is packed with kids, parents, siblings anything you can imagine. Someone can get hurt in a moment's notice. Again, the goal is to hand them off to the coaches and let them go to warms ups in one piece. Only this year it was different, as Team Dad I was going to go with the coaches to assist with the team. I was actually pretty excited about this. I had already adopted this group as my own. I was curious to see what happens that makes these kids so focused and dialed in when they come out on stage.

It was almost time and the team started to get really excited. As Coach Kelsey gave the order to take off warm-ups it was time. For a parent, the phase "Ok warm ups off" is your cue. That is your last time to get you child organized, last touch ups for make-up hugs, kisses etc... Everyone was ready. Coach Kelsey and Coach Jessica were leading the team down to warm ups as Coach Ashley was still with the Grape Rays. As the team assembled and began to hold hands with one another, I noticed something. As all the girls were lining up two by two. I noticed my man Beecher was a little hesitant. You see this is a mini team. So the boy / girl thing was still being worked out in the prepubescent stage of their lives. He may have felt a little unintentionally left out.

Well I could certainly relate to how Beecher was feeling. As I looked around, I was clearly the only Team Dad in the room. So I walked over to Beecher and said "Why don't you and I go to the back of the group, and us dudes can make sure these nice ladies make it safely to warm ups." Beecher looked up at me relieved, put on a huge smile and said "that sounds like a good idea." As we walked to warm ups bringing up the back of the group, I knew I made a new friend in Beecher.

It was time. We made it to our pre warm up staging area. This is where the team starts prepping for warm ups, but it is really a time the team begins getting their head in the game. With a young group it is critical to have a consistent routine. The coaches are masterful at getting the team prepared. What was astounding to me was how all these young athletes burnt off their nervous energy. These kids really get excited to go on stage. They work so hard for so long and now it was time. They could feel it. The few minutes before warm ups consist of the opening, working on buddy stunts and other stunt group drills. In between drills is chaos, all born out of nervous energy. There is laughter (tons of it) crying, jumping tumbling, etc... I was amazed at the composure of the coaches because I was a nervous mess. As the team made its way back to warm ups the coaches stated that they did not need my assistance in the warm up area as Coach Ashley was going to make it back in time from Grape.

I gave the team hugs and high fives and scurried out to the viewing area to get ready to watch the Grape Rays light up the stage. As Grape was about to go on I saw Coach Ashley taking her position as Grape was about to hit the stage. I told her that Peppermint was looking great and were ready to go. That put her at ease for only a second as she shifted her focus to Grape. The Grape Rays completed a fantastic routine for their first time on the stage. They did go on to win the competition which was the second year in a row Grape had won at Encore.

Encore is a one day competition. Most of the competitions Stingrays competes in are two day competitions. The scary thing about a one day competition is there is no room for error. If you drop, tumble-bust or bobble it could cost you the competition. As they say in All Star cheer, "If you "hit" you just might win. If you don't you could expect to lose". You get one shot in a two minute thirty second routine to show the judges what you got!

As we watched the other mini teams competing, I noticed some good competition. All of the teams put together great routines and I was very impressed. As I watched more teams, I started to get nervous. Was our routine to ambitious? Are they going to hit that tough stunt? What am I going to tell my daughter if they do not hit? All of these thoughts run through my head as a parent of an All Star Cheerleader. It can be very stressful making sure you are supportive at all times and be a leader for your child no matter what happens. Emotions run high, and everyone wants their kids' team to win. While winning is nice, it was important for my wife and I to instill that they "do their best" and that is all we will ask of them.

As Peppermint came on stage, I noticed they had a swagger about them. After watching the team for almost seven months I could tell when they were on their game. As the coaches came out and were getting settled in front of the team, I quickly asked Coach Kelsey how they looked in warm ups. She gave me a concerning look and said it was a mess. A few of the parents leaned over to me to ask me what Coach Kelsey said. I responded, "She said they looked incredible!" I learned very quickly last year that the team will respond to the parents in the viewing area. The kids know when something is not right. It can be a gesture or a grim look on a parents face that can send a routine into a tizzy. We have strict rules as a parent group. No matter what happens in the routine keep the energy high and a smiling face the entire time as team feeds off the energy good or bad.

The routine started and Peppermint hit the opening with a bang. They had great energy and were very crisp and clean. As the routine went on they got even better. Peppermint performed with tons of confidence and an energy that was off the charts. This was the beginning of something special, we could all feel it. As the team assembled into the "stunt of death" none of the stunt groups batted an eye. They nailed the stunt perfectly. They went on to hit the pyramid sequence flawlessly and the dance was incredible. After the music ended the team erupted on stage as they knew they hit! As the parents started to filter off to assemble to wait for the team, a few parents from random teams at the competition came over to compliment how the routine went. They were very impressed. That rarely happens with a Level 1 mini team.

A few hours passed and it was time for awards. All of the Level 1 teams had all performed from the Tiny division (4/5 yr. olds) all the way to the senior Level 1 division (High School age). In all, there were about sixty level 1 teams that performed on that day total. I was nervous as there were some great teams that competed. We had just learned that Grape finished in first place which I was happy about. Now it was time to find out how Peppermint finished.

They announce the team placements in reverse order. As the 4th place and 3rd place team were announced, we knew we were in the top two. As the anticipation was building the MC announced the second place team. At that point we knew. Peppermint finished in FIRST! We were all very excited. We got the fifth place monkey off our back and I had two daughters going home with first place medals.

As we started to pack our stuff and get our kids organized. The MC started to announce that they would be announcing the Grand Champion of the competition momentarily. As the parent of a Tiny and a Mini team we normally just disregard that announcement as many times a Youth, Junior or Senior team normally win Grand Champion. Well this time that changed. The MC announced "And your Grand Champion for Level 1 goes to "From Marietta Georgia The Stingray Allstars Peppermint!" My wife Kelly looked at me and said, "Did he just say Peppermint?" I said, "Yes I think he did." Sure enough they won Grand Champion of Level 1 which equates to the best routine of all Level 1 teams that competed no matter what the age. We knew the routine was incredible, but the judges validated the performance with the award. It was a great start to the competition season.

First Place at Encore

The First Grand Champion Award of the Season

6 WSF LOUISVILLE KENTUCKY

A few weeks later it was time for the World Spirit Federation Competition in Louisville, KY. This competition is huge. Last year there were teams from all over the nation that descended to Louisville. My daughters had incredible memories from the previous year competition as it falls a few weeks before Christmas and the city does an incredible job welcoming the Cheer Nation as they take over the city for a weekend. The Stingray Allstars Tiny and Mini teams had quite a bit to prove this year. While Peppermint struggled in the previous year at Encore and finished 5th, they bounced back and came to Louisville in 2013 and won Grand Champion at WSF which was a remarkable accomplishment, and showed the resilience of that team. The Grape Rays also came away with a win against some very stiff competition.

In Kentucky they take their cheerleading very seriously. The University of Kentucky and Louisville have always had one of the best college cheerleading teams in the nation for many years. They have many extremely talented All Star teams in the state and they all converge on Louisville for this competition. There is quite a bit at stake.

The older teams (Youth level and up) will be competing for at large bids and full paid bids for Summit and Worlds. At this competition, our open teams the Electric Rays were going to compete against some of the best teams in the world. Electric is a team of college level athletes and coaches from the area. The team competes in the Open Level 5 division and they attempt some of the most amazing stunts and tumbling you will ever see. Many of the coaches from Stingrays compete on Electric which makes it very exciting for the kids to watch. Bottom line is, the competition is huge and very important.

For those of you who are not familiar with Tiny and Mini All Star Cheer. The day starts with a 4:45 am wake-up call to get your child up and ready to perform. Most of the younger teams go on between 8 am and 10 am in the morning. You can do the math. With a forty five minute warm up time before competition, and time needed to get the team organized and ready, you need every ounce of time you can get before the team competes. Most normal people will never understand why cheer parents do what we do for this sport. That is ok, we understand, we love it, our kids love it, we are a unique group of families and we all have each other's back.

As we arrive at the convention center at 5:45 am sharp. The place was mass hysteria. I knew this was a large competition, but this year was different. They announced this year was the largest WSF competition ever and I could tell. The parent texts for Peppermint started flying early for this competition as traffic was an issue (yes at 5:45 am) and the convention center is huge. I was a bit more comfortable at this competition as a Team Dad as I had the first one under my belt. The team started filtering in and the kids were energetic as ever. Coach Kelsey arrived in her uniform. She was going to be performing with the Electric Rays on that day. Then Coach Jessica showed in her uniform she was going to be performing with the Frost Rays on that day. Then Coach Rupert showed in his uniform he was also on Electric. While most of the Mint's arrived we had a few that were running late that I had not communicated with. While sometimes that happens the reality is, if there is no communication my mind automatically goes to the worst case scenario which is, "They are oversleeping and did not wake up in time!" This happens more often than you might imagine, and with a team sport it can be very challenging to fill the spot of a missing teammate on a moments notice.

Luckily the final teammate walked in and everyone was accounted for. Coach Kelsey asked if I would help with the team in warm ups. I said absolutely! She said, "Are you sure you are ready for this?" as she gave me a grin. I said, "I will do my best." As the announcement was made to take off warm ups, Peppermint seemed very loose and confident. This team was becoming very tight and they all had each other's backs you could tell. As the convention center was lined with literally thousands of people and other cheer teams, Peppermint lined up as they normally do and we started to make our way to warm ups. As I was getting my stuff organized, I noticed over my shoulder I had someone waiting on me to go with the team. I heard the team yell "come on Mr. Eric!" Beecher was waiting for me and the team did not want to leave without me. So I ran, caught up with Beecher and we escorted the team down to warm ups. It was our new thing.

After pre-warm up we made our way into the official warm up room. This was my first time as a parent to be back there. It was amazing, hundreds of teams and thousands of kids tumbling, stunting and dancing with grace and precision all within inches of each other. It was mid-morning and many of the older senior level teams were starting to filter back to the area. I was caught staring in awe of all the teams. I could have easily got lost in all the chaos. Peppermint lined up against the wall in order to make sure we had everyone. It is very easy to get distracted amongst all the teams. The biggest challenge is making sure your team is together and do not wonder off as many teams go full out. A wandering child can collide with another tumbling child. I really had to stay focused on the kids and where they were at all times.

We had a few minutes before our assigned time in warm ups. The teams are assigned a specific time to use, and if you are late you just flat out lose your time. We had about 15 minutes before we went back to warm ups. Coach Kelsey mentioned it was time to take the team to the restroom and she would need my help. Then she said oh wait … you're a guy. Awkward moment number one for me, obviously I could not help with the seventeen other female cheerleaders to expedite the process of buttoning up uniforms. I asked if we were going to have enough time to get all eighteen of them in and out of the restroom in time for warm ups. She smiled and said "I got this." Without going into much detail, lets just say the uniform had a very challenging area to button up. As Beecher and I waited for the group, the most important thing I could do was distribute hand sanitizer. To my amazement, Coach Kelsey got all seventeen cheerleaders in and out of the restroom in nine minutes flat!

The team headed to warm ups as confident as ever. They were surrounded by some of the best teams in the nation from gyms that are household names to those of us that follow the sport. This competition clearly had some great teams and Peppermint was excited to be a part of it. They jumped onto the mats and began their opening. The coaches were demanding excellence and precision. The team was looking amazing. They went through the "stunt of death" sequence and then I noticed something began to happen. In the background, some of the other teams and coaches from other programs started to drift over to watch Peppermint practice. As the team went through their routine more and more people were coming over to watch them. Youth teams, senior teams, other mini teams. I started to count and noticed five other teams and coaches watching Peppermint warm up. The kids were unfazed, but it was something I noticed and thought was odd. When a mini team begins to turn heads from other programs you have something special going on.

Coach Ashley returned from coaching Grape and she picked right up with the intensity level that our other Mint coaches were bringing. With eighteen other mini teams competing in this competition, this was no joke, and everyone had to be on their game. As we progressed through warm ups the team began to struggle. I think the adrenaline and excitement was beginning to wear on the team. The easiest skill began to be a challenge. Coach Ashley noticed they were out of synch and told them to take a break and go get some water. After the break they came back re-focused but they were still off quite a bit. As I was in the back, one of the parents texted me to ask how the team looked in warm ups, as I was watching stunts fall and the dance was out of sequence I typed out. "They look absolutely incredible".

Peppermint walked hand in hand together to line up and get ready to take the stage. The moment behind stage is indescribable. The nervous energy is amazing. It is a time where the team composes itself, begins to focus and visualize the routine they have been working on for seven months. Coach Ashley started to get the team together. I stepped back and watched in amazement while she spoke with the team. "Ok, this is our time to set the pace for this competition. We need to come out strong and show these teams that we mean business. All I ask is that you do your best, that's all I ask. No matter what happens out there, all I ask is that you keep pushing through the whole routine and I promise we will be happy with the outcome." We lined the team up and sprayed them with the famous "lucky spray" and left them with the security and another Stingray representative behind stage. I gave my daughter a little hug and we were off. I was shocked we just kind of left them. It was only a minute or two but it seemed like an eternity. I asked Coach Kelsey if that was normal and she said "Yep, they need this time alone as a group."

We made our way to the front of the stage. I made eye contact with my wife and she and the other Peppermint parents packed in behind us. As we were packing in, all of a sudden we noticed a few other Stingray teams scrambling in the preferred viewing area to watch Peppermint. It was a few athletes from Peach and Orange! Some of the teams snuck away from pre-warm up to come and watch and root for the Mints. The Peppermint parents noticed and started pointing to all of the Senior 5 teams that were showing up to watch. It was an incredible feeling of love and support for the senior teams to come down and watch our team.

When the curtain opened and the Mints ran on stage, they noticed their parents first, and then you could tell, the Mints noticed the Senior 5 teams that had assembled to watch. As they lined up for the music to start, you could tell by looks of confidence on their face. IT WAS ON! The music started and they completed a flawless routine. The "Stunt of Death" shocked the arena and the crowd was amazed by the energy.

After the team performance they assembled in the back to watch their routine. After a "hit" the team is riding on an enormous emotional high. The group begins to watch the replay of the routine on the monitor. They go over it with a fine tooth comb and critique it together as a team. There were a few very minor flaws but other than that they nailed it. The team came flying out from behind stage pumped they knew they did great. My daughter came and gave me a huge flying hug. The first thing she said to me was "Did you see that Peach and Orange came to watch us?" Peppermint was all a buzz about the "Big Kids" coming to watch them it meant a lot to them.

We went back to the hotel to wait for the day 1 results. After waiting a few hours Coach Ashley sent me a text that out of nineteen teams after day 1 we were in first place! The entire group was pumped. I sent the text out to all the parents and it was electric. In a two day competition the most important thing you can do as a Tiny/ Mini parents is get your child to sleep early. It is a tough task as all of the parents and mints were so fired up. After watching Peach, Orange and Electric perform your adrenaline kicks in and you want to stay up all night.

Day two begins and we are back in warm ups. As we start going through the routine something is severely off with the group. The team is not focused and they are dropping the easiest parts of the routine. They begin to get better about halfway through warm ups but they are not on their game. I noticed more and more teams coming to watch them warm up. It is about this time the Coach Ashley arrives. She notices they are not sharp and crisp. She begins to coach them. After talking with them for about ten minutes the team progressed over to the "full out" area where the teams can walk through their entire routine and set it to their music. It is the final five minutes of warm up before you head toward lining up to go on stage. They looked better but they were still off a bit.

We grouped up and started walking back stage. While we were walking we had a group waiting for us behind stage. As the team got closer, we recognized the group cheering us on, it was Stingray PEACH! The Peppermints exploded with excitement. Most of the team ran to see Peach; they gave hugs and great words of encouragement. It was exactly what Peppermint needed to get their head back in the game. After the group mingled with Peach, Coach Ashley assembled the group and started to get the team focused and delivered an inspiring message before the team went on the stage for Day 2. The team was already jacked about Peach cheering them on. Coach Ashley said "Ok it's YOUR time! It's time to show these people who you are. I know you guys can be the best Mini team in the WORLD if you go out and do your best. That is all I am going to ask of you. You do your best and let's show all these people who the best mini team in the WORLD is!" With that the coaches doused the team with lucky spray. It was a team ritual, you probably would not understand.

As the team was about to go on stage we had quite a few more viewers on Day 2. The atmosphere is electric on the second day as all the teams are pressing for that perfect routine. Everyone knew that Peppermint was on top after day one. Many folks wanted to see what the buzz was about, but a lot of people were there to see if this team could hit this ambitious routine two days in row.

As Peppermint took the stage, I could see the team had a look about them. They came out strong and the facials and the attitude was amazing. This team lived for their moment on stage. This was their time to shine and they were doing it again. It was hard to believe only thirty short minutes ago they could barely string together a tumble pass.

The switch was turned on! They came out of their pyramid and the entire front group stomped on the floor in sequence unrehearsed. They finished the dance flawlessly. They left the floor ecstatic as they knew that they did what Coach Ashley asked of them. They did their best and they knew it! They "Hit" again and the place went bananas.

As the team assembled to watch the video of their performance as they left the stage a few of the girls were crying tears of joy. My eight year old daughter was one of them. She came over to me in tears and gave me a huge hug. She said "Daddy, I don't know why I am crying, but I am so happy we did our best." This was a moment I cherished as a Dad. I attempted to explain to her what "tears of joy" meant. Up to this point, I was very careful to make sure I treated my daughter just like all of the teammates. I was careful not to show any preferential treatment. In this moment, I let my guard down. I was ok with that.

As the award ceremony approached, I was to help assemble the team for awards as usual. The team was busting at the seams with excitement. Typically a squad never gets to watch the other eighteen teams that compete. They may be able to see one or two teams in front of them while they are waiting to go on stage, but more often than not, they can only hope that they performed their best and hope they outshined the competition. The other Peppermint parents watched most all of the other teams that performed. A few were nervous because the teams that were in second and third place on day one performed well.

While I escorted the team back to the award ceremony they were all bouncing around and excited. For as confident as this group is, they were also a very humble group of kids. We assembled in our two lines and Beecher came by my side and started asking a few questions. He seemed a little nervous as this was a very big arena and there were a ton of people entering the convention center for awards. Beecher looked up at me and asked, "Are all these people coming to watch our award ceremony?" He seemed very intimidated and intrigued by the large group gathering for awards. I said, "Yup buddy they sure are." He took another look out at all the people he turned back to me and asked me if they did ok?" I said, "I think so, but there are eighteen other really great teams here so we will have to see." Beecher answered "Well, we did our best, that's all we can do." I smiled and said, "You sure did buddy and I am really proud of you guys."

As the MC started announcing the teams in reverse order the Peppermints were getting anxious to hear where they finished. The anticipation grew as we made it into the final five teams. The third and fourth place teams were announced and everyone politely clapped for the other teams as Mint was excited to make into the top five. It was truly a huge accomplishment. Peppermint was getting noticeably nervous as the final two teams were announced. The MC built up the intensity level and excitement for the final time. The 2nd place team was announced and we then knew.

The MC gave the second place team an opportunity to pick up their banner and celebrate their accomplishment. He then announced, "And your winner from Marietta, Georgia the Stingray Allstars Peppermint!" The team flew up off the mat and began to celebrate. They were pumped, and they deserved it. The team walked up to receive their banner to a resounding round of applause.

After the teams cleared the floor, Peppermints were instructed to go to the champions area behind the stage to get their National Champions Jackets and medals. I helped escort the team behind the stage. The coaches helped keep the team somewhat organized but they were jacked! All of the coaches had to leave as they had other teams and responsibilities. It was me and eighteen extremely excited kids and some security officers.

They had questions, tons of questions. Before warm ups on day two Coach Ashley shared that Peppermint did extremely well on Day one. She went on to share the teams score and how they could improve on the score for Day two. She also said if the team did their best again. They had a good chance of being "Grand Champion" for Level 1 again like they did at Encore. That is all the team wanted to discuss. Mr. Eric do you think we did good enough to win Grand Champion? We won it last year! Do you think we can do it again this year?" They were on cloud nine and bouncing off the walls.

As the team lined up to take pictures and receive their medals they focused on what they accomplished on the day. Little did they know that the Grand Champion for Level 1 announcement was not scheduled to happen for another five hours. The competition was so large it took that long to get through all the Youth, Junior, and Senior Level 1 teams. It was going to be a long seven hour drive back to Marietta, so we headed back as the kids had school the following day. On the drive back, twitter was our savior. We almost broke our thumbs trying to refresh Twitter. The entire drive my wife was announcing who won. There was a huge wave of Stingray teams she announced. We were almost home from Louisville when the picture popped up. Peppermint took the Level 1 Grand Champion of WSF back to back!

Grand Champion Level 1 WSF Kentucky

7 ATHLETIC CHAMPIONSHIPS

Peppermint was riding a huge wave after WSF. Actually, the entire gym was. The Stingray All-Stars completely dominated the entire event from Level 1 all the way to Senior 5 along with our IOC5 team Electric who won a paid bid to Worlds along with a few other Senior teams. It was a great weekend for all the teams. The following day it was back to the gym for more practice and tumble. You would think after a long drive back home and school the following day the kids would be beat. The truth is, after you win a six foot tall Grand Champion trophy you want to see it in the gym and share it with your team, friends and family. It was back to work for Peppermint. As the team started to filter into the gym some of the teammates were all chatting amongst themselves and showing each other their first place medals. Many of the Mints wanted to take a picture with the Grand Champion trophy as they were very proud of their accomplishment.

As the teams began to practice they began their normal routine. Walking through and marking the counts. Their big sisters from Peach started filtering into the gym and as they entered Peppermint got a water break. Many of the Mints found a few of the Peach teammates and gave hugs and congratulations on their big win at WSF. Peach looked very strong and the girls were bonding over their accomplishments. It was fun to watch the comradery between the two teams grow. This was the second year in a row that Peppermint had won Grand Champion at WSF. To say that was impressive was an understatement and a testament to the coaching staff.

The #minniemintsandmickey was becoming a "thing" in the gym. Coach Ashley had the vision to label this team as such, and it was a perfect label in more ways than one. The team prepared for the next competition coming up in Chattanooga, TN. The team was very confident as they were riding the high from WSF. Coach Ashley worked hard to make sure the group of kids stayed grounded and focused. With children as young as this team was, that is a very hard thing to do.

As the last practice before Chattanooga began, the team looked spectacular. They were wrapping up their last round of Full Outs and they "Hit" three in a row. It was a great final practice to end on. The team was confident for our upcoming trip. Peppermint families loaded up and headed north for the weekend.

Chattanooga is a great city for a competition. It is a quaint city with tons of charm and very welcoming for families. There is a ton to do for kids in a very close proximity. They have buggy rides, children's museums, a beautiful aquarium, great restaurants, and haunted mystery tours.

As we arrived in Chattanooga one of my responsibilities as Team Dad is making sure all of the Peppermints arrive safely at our destination and all team members are accounted for. Since Chattanooga was such a short drive for most of us, I was relieved as all of the teams and families arrived early and checked in quickly. We as a family check into the historic "Reed House" in Chattanooga. The hotel is a staple in the city and has a ton of history. We stayed in the hotel the previous year and really enjoyed the property. We booked it again this year and as we arrived to check in we were pleasantly surprised that the front desk upgraded our room to a larger suite. As we started to move our luggage into the room, I received the final text and confirmed everyone was safely in Chattanooga. Normally, a city with a longer travel distance families will run into traffic, flight delays, etc. It can be a late night waiting for people to arrive. Tonight was an exception and a good friend and I decided to grab some dinner at the hotel restaurant as the entire team was accounted for.

My wife and kids decided not to join us as they wanted to get a good night sleep. One of the most important things you can do at a competition with a Tiny and Mini cheerleader is make sure your kids get to bed at a decent hour, as waking up on the wrong side of the bad can spell disaster. On the way down to the restaurant one of the Grape Rays came screaming and crying down the hall. She was completely hysterical. She was running toward our room and alerted me that there were ghosts in the hotel and that we had had ghosts in our room. I calmed the little grape ray down and assured her there were no ghosts in our room, and that she should go find her mom and start getting ready for bed. My daughters were getting settled in for bed, and I did not want her to scare them by sharing a ghost story right before bed.

Part of the charm of Chattanooga is that they advertise "Haunted Hotel" tours. They do a great job with them and the Reed House hotel is part of the popular tours. I thought nothing more of the situation and headed down to meet Louis at the hotel restaurant. We had a great time and dinner and I returned upstairs after a few hours to turn in for the night. When I arrived to the room, my wife Kelly was frustrated to say the least. She said multiple people had been banging on the door all night and it was waking up the kids. I said, "Well it's a cheer competition and it is probably just kids trying to be funny knocking on the door and running off." My wife replied, "I think it has something to do with the Haunted Hotel scenario." My thoughts immediately went to the hysterical Grape Ray that was coming down the hall to warn us about our room. I did not think much more about it.

About five minutes later I heard a violent banging on the door. BAM, BAM, BAM, BAM. I shot up out of bed and headed toward the door. I could hear people talking and laughing outside our door. I opened the door and the group ran down the hall screaming as if they did not expect the door to open. One of the kids said "Mister did you know you are in the haunted room? We were just coming to check it out?" I closed the door and came back to bed. I jumped on my phone and googled, "Haunted Hotels Chattanooga". On top of the search results was "The Reed House" I went on to read, "The famous haunting of room 311". You guessed it; we were "UPGRADED" to room 311 for the night. As I finished the article there was another bang on the door. I ran as fast as I could to open the door so the noise did not wake up the sleeping girls. I swung the door open and to my surprise the teenager staring me right in the face did not run off. He looked straight at me, and asked if he could come in the room and look around. The look I gave the kid must have turned the light on in his head, as he quickly scurried down the hallway toward the elevator. I closed the door went into the bedroom and got dressed. I was going down to speak with the manager to get us moved to another room ASAP.

On the way down to the lobby, I was so frustrated about the situation that I jumped on the elevator going up. I was greeted by an overly nice couple who seemed to have been pretty inebriated. The wife began to chat with me and asked me, "Do you think it is crazy if my husband is milling around a hotel that we are not even staying in to find the haunted room in this hotel?" I did not immediately respond. She could tell I was a little frustrated by something. I waited about a minute and stated, "I don't think that would be a very good idea. The room you are looking for is the one I am currently staying in and I have two young daughters who are trying to sleep and every five minutes someone starts banging on the door!" The couple apologized and was so flustered they got off the elevator on the top floor. I may have made them a bit uncomfortable. As they got off, another lady jumped on at the top floor. She very politely asked, "How is your evening going?" I replied, "I have had better." I explained our haunted room situation and told the lady that I was headed to the front desk to speak with someone. She looked down at the floor and calmly said, "Well I think the person you are coming to speak with is me I am the night manager." She was so embarrassed by the entire thing. The hotel did a great job in remedying the situation as they placed security on the floor and placed a sign outside of our room. We did not have another disturbance for the rest of the evening, and were moved to another room the following night.

The Famous Haunted Room in Chattanooga

The next morning my wife and I were exhausted, luckily the girls slept right through everything. The good news was that Peppermint looked like they were ready to go. The entire team was in a great mood and they were eager to take the floor for day one. Peppermint was riding a wave from the last couple of competitions and wanted to set the tone. Going into warm ups the vibe was good and they headed off.

As the mints came out on stage to perform, I noticed the energy level was not what it usually is. They seemed a little off. As the routine progressed, there were a few bobbles and the routine was not as clean as it normally would be. The team finished the routine strong and it was a great effort, but not as clean and confident as usual. As we learned later that day Peppermint was in first place after Day one but they had a ton of room for improvement. The second place team was right on their heels. Peppermint needed to come out with the confidence and energy they normally do to win this competition.

Day two was among us and they team seemed very loose. So far, this was their first real test of the season. I was interested to see how they would respond knowing they were not the clear favorite going into day two.

For six, seven, and eight year old kids this team performed incredibly well under pressure. Mint was getting ready to leave for warm ups and they were having a great time together as they normally do. Last minute prep and make up application before we heard the words, "Alright warm ups off". The group left for warm ups and the parent group cheered loudly to pump them up.

When they hit the stage, I knew immediately. The music started and they came out with attitude and spunk. They hit the "Stunt of death" with vigor and the facials and stomps were out in full force. Peppermint was on fire! They were not going to be denied on this day. They finished the routine and flew off stage with confidence. They knew they finished well, now it was just up to the other teams. Hopefully Peppermint did not get outshined on this day.

As we waited for awards I was as nervous as usual. With two daughters I want both of their teams to do well. More importantly, I hope they both finish in the same place it does not have to be first place, just the same place. It just makes life easier. While my daughters are best friends and play and love each other fiercely. They do like to press each other's buttons when one wins and one does not. The sibling rivalry is real and it can get ugly. As we awaited the fate of the Peppermint Rays we found out that the Grape Rays won first place. I breathed a sigh of relief as we now began to wait for the announcement of the Mini Level division. As the teams were announced we moved into the top three teams. As the second place team was announced, we then knew. The Minnie Mints and Mickey were still undefeated and they did it again! We won the Athletic Championships for the third year in a row!

The two day performance was not their best of the season but they finished great. The focus now shifted as the team wondered if they would become Grand Champion for the third competition in a row. As the day progressed, it was evident it would not be in the cards. The Grand Champion for Level 1 was announced and it was not Peppermint.

As practice resumed, the team was disappointed they did not win Grand Champion. In my opinion, it was just what the team needed to regroup and re focus. They were on the verge of doing something special as a mini team. Twitter began to buzz about how good this group was becoming. I was seeing tweets from people all over who heard about the team, and how good the routine was. It was fun to see the chatter about a mini team. Of course, the team was completely oblivious to all of this, as none of them had social media accounts.

Coach Ashley got the team back to work and also took the time to explain why they did not win Grand Champion for the previous competition. She explained how hard it was to win Grand Champion and if they wanted to do it again they would need to keep practicing, do their best and hope the judges saw all the hard work they were putting in at practice. That week of practice was the most dialed in I have seen the team to date. Every full out was a "hit". The energy was contagious and the bond between Peach and Mint continued to grow as they went full out for each other and pushed each other to take it to the next level.

The next competition was the Cheersport regionals in Atlanta, Georgia. Stingrays affectionately refer to the competition as "Little Cheersport" which is a one day competition that gets the entire gym tuned up for the next huge competition which is the Cheersport Nationals which is arguably the biggest competition in the world. Peppermint was completely dialed in for this competition. From the beginning of the day you could tell they wanted to make up for the less than perfect performance from the Athletic Championships. You could tell Peppermint had a bit of a chip on their shoulder not being selected as Grand Champion from the previous competition. The coaching staff had them completely focused and ready.

As the team headed back for warm up, I noticed a few familiar faces that started to gather to watch Peppermint. With Cheersport being held in Atlanta, there were many Stingray alumni and athletes from other gyms who wanted to catch a glimpse of the mini team people were talking about. We also noticed the support the rest of the gym was providing, as many familiar faces from other Stingray teams were coming to watch the "Mini Mints and Mickey". It was so flattering to see the incredible Level 5 athletes from Stingrays coming to cheer on our minis.

As the team hit the stage they had a fierce look about them. Coach Ashley was expecting a great performance from them and they wanted to deliver. They came out of the gates flawless with a ton of energy. As the team went into their stunt transition you could tell everything was immaculate and effortless. The team then picked up momentum into the pyramid and nailed it, the jumps and dance were flawless. After the routine, the parents were buzzing. I personally was shocked at how good their performance was. It was breathtaking, and I was astounded by the execution and cleanliness. I have seen some clean routines in my three years watching Stingray teams, but this routine was special. The team knew they did well, and was buzzing with excitement. The parents greeted the group with huge hugs as Coach Ashley gave some final words of encouragement and was proud that they did their best and gave a great effort.

As the awards announcements were being made. We found out that the Minnie Mints and Mickey did it again. They won first place! The team was ecstatic. As Team Dad, I was instructed to get the team organized for pictures and release the children to their parents. While we were patiently waiting for our pictures, one of the staff officials handed the scoring packet to the Peppermint coaching staff. Coach Kelsey and Coach Jessica opened the scoresheet and both of their jaws literally hit the floor. They both covered their mouths looking at the score sheet. I asked, "How did they do?" they looked over at me and said "Well I can't tell you the score, but let me tell you, it is one of the best scores I have seen in a very long time." Needless to say the Peppermints went on to win their third Grand Champion for the year!

Grand Champion Little Cheersport

8 PREPARING FOR THE BIG 3

All the Stingray All Star teams headed back to the gym. It was another great showing for all the Stingrays including Peppermint. The next three competitions are the ones you prepare for the entire season. All competitions are critical, but the next three are the most important. It can make or break your season. For older teams, the pressure gets ramped up as all Stingray teams want to win an at large bid or a paid bid to Summit or Worlds. For those who are unaware. Worlds are an invitation only event that represents the best Senior Level All Star Cheer squads in the world. For non-senior level teams everyone is shooting for an at large or paid bid to the Summit which is a similar competition for youth and up aged teams that are not Level 5.

Cheersport which is held in Atlanta, Georgia is one of the largest competitions in the world. This competition is hosted at the Georgia World Congress Center and takes over the entire downtown area of Atlanta. This competition hosts literally thousands of Cheer teams from all over the world. It is a big deal for all teams especially Stingrays as this is really our home competition. Cheersport offers thirty bids for over a thousand cheer squads so the competition is fierce. The pressure starts to build as Cheersport looms ahead. Right after Cheersport the cheer nation focuses on the next big competition which is NCA. This competition is held in Dallas, TX and is arguably just as big and as important as Cheersport.

NCA is considered by most as the granddaddy of them all. Winning an NCA jacket is one of the most coveted accomplishments, outside of winning Summit or Worlds. After NCA comes UCA which is held at the ESPN Wide World of Sports in Orlando, FL while UCA is not as big as Cheersport or NCA it is often one of the team and family favorites to attend for obvious reasons.

The Big three as we refer to them at Stingrays is the final time for the older teams to show what they are made of and earn a bid to Summit and Worlds. The competition is tough as you will see all year and everyone is competing to take you out. Everyone wants the bids, the jackets and the medals. This is one of the final three competitions to get it done. As if that was not enough, Varsity added another prestigious element to the Big 3 called the Triple Crown.

The Triple Crown was established to recognize participants in all three of the Varsity competitions. The point race extends to all ages and all divisions. You must compete in Cheersport, NCA and UCA and the team that finishes with the best point total for all three wins a really nice prize package and a banner to hang in your respective gym to recognize your accomplishments. You can also win the Triple Crown outright by winning all three events in your division. Most importantly, it is the ultimate bragging rights to say you competed against the very best competition and ended up on top.

Since Peppermint was a mini team, the kids and the parents did not have to worry about the added stress of winning a Summit Bid. The team did not qualify due to age, as Summit Bids are awarded to youth teams (nine, ten and eleven year olds) and higher. Peppermints team goal was to be in the running for the Triple Crown. It would be an incredible accomplishment for the team and would really give them a story they would treasure forever. Winning the Triple Crown would be no easy task. We as a parent group whispered about the possibility amongst ourselves, but never spoke of the Triple Crown in front of our kids as we are all a very superstitious group.

More importantly, I think the parents knew we were watching something develop that was very special. The team, coaches and the parents were all part of building a group that defined the word team. To me, there is nothing more important than watching your children grow into leaders, be coachable, and treat all of your teammates equally while working together to achieve one goal. It is what defines all successful teams. It is what we were watching when we looked out at Peach when they were practicing. It is what Peppermint was modeling both from watching Peach and Orange but also the incredible leadership of the Peppermint coaching staff. Heading into the biggest competitions of the year, this team did not want to let their coaches or each other down. There were only a few days left before the first leg of the triple-crown. Cheersport week was here, and it was time to dial it in.

As a mini team, the innocence and naiveté was showing. Being young and innocent has its advantages, to Peppermint Cheersport was just another competition. What became so special looking back on this season was the spirit of the entire team. They approached each competition just as the previous. It did not matter to them how big of a stage they were about to go on. They took it one competition at a time. I know it sounds cliché but Peppermint not only lived for the pressure, they thrived in it. Up to this point, the group had been nonchalantly strolling through this season flawlessly. They were focusing on their routine, strong coaching and each other. Nothing else mattered. The final week before Cheersport flew by. It did not seem we had enough time to get everything perfect. The last day of practice was upon us and it was time to shine.

As the teams gathered for practice, Peppermint knew that there would be a heavy dose of full out parties in preparation for Cheersport. Full out parties include multiple teams gathering to cheer each other on as they go full out for all the other teams and coaches at Stingrays. The exercise achieves multiple things. While you can never duplicate the pressure of going out on stage at a competition, full out parties ramp up the intensity level and pressure to look flawless in front of other Stingray teams.

As Peppermint was progressing through practice they walked and marked the routine. They worked through some of their stunts, jumps and pyramid. You could tell they were getting ready to go full out. You could see the excitement and nervous energy from the parents viewing area. The teams began to gather at the front mat. It was the usual suspects Peppermint, Mango and Peach. As Peach headed toward the mat the teams erupted in excitement you could feel the love all the way up in the viewing area. As Peach started their routine, Peppermint was glued to their every move. They knew the routine almost as well as Peach. They hung on every stunt sequence. As Peach went into their Elite Stunt you could see the Peppermints bopping up and down because they knew their favorite part of the routine was coming up. As the music blasted Peppermint leaned in poised to scream at the top of their little lungs. I began to smirk because I knew what was coming. In unison, the Mints belted out "I GOT 99 PROBLEMS BUT A PEACH AIN'T ONE!!" of course this is one of the iconic voice overs from the 2014-2015 Peach routine that will live on in infamy. Peach finished up their dance and nailed another hit.

Peppermint ran out onto the mat next. They were so excited to go after Peach. It was really neat to see the parents from other teams wanting to stay and watch Peppermint go full out. The parents would also recruit parents from other teams to come over to watch Peppermint go full out. It was such an incredible feeling to have the support from other teams. It is what makes Stingrays such a special place. We as a parent group tried to return the favor whenever possible.

As the routine began, Peppermint got off to a strong start. The opening was clean as they began progressing toward the "Stunt of Death." They made it through the stunt with no problems. After watching Peach they wanted to be great. After observing the team for the past eight months three times a week, I could tell the routine was off. Sometimes it's the energy level, sometimes it's the timing. This time I could tell the timing was off a bit. The team progressed into the pyramid and we had a few bobbles in the pyramid. The dance was fine, but the team knew they did not hit, and the energy was not there.

Peppermint finished and you could tell the team was disappointed in their performance. Peach did not miss a beat and yelled and screamed anyway as they always did for all the teams. Coach Ashley briefly spoke to the team. As I was up in the viewing area of course I could not tell you exactly what she said but I am guessing it was along the lines of, " We do not want to end the night on that one, lets show Peach what we are made of." Peppermint regrouped after the other teams completed their full outs. They started the second time and immediately I knew they were dialed in. The last full out finished flawlessly. Peach erupted with cheers as did the other teams supporting the Mints. Coach Ashley gave a smirk and a little nod to the team. She knew they were ready.

Building your strategy to plan for Cheersport as a family is truly a logistical marvel. The Georgia World Congress center has its own zip code for a reason. When over 1200 cheer teams descend on a competition the goal is to deflect any drama or challenges and keep everyone as calm as possible. To say the competition is huge is an understatement. If you let it, the competition can consume you. A strict and tight process is the best way to attack Cheersport. Thankfully, it was not our first rodeo as a family.

Arrive super early and stay loose is the best plan of attack. This was my first competition as a Team Dad. My goal was to try and make the families who were experiencing Cheersport for the first time as comfortable as possible. Comfortable parents equal loose and confident cheerleaders. Thankfully, everyone arrived early and the entire team began playing together as they always do. Before warm ups the vibe was great. We did have a few kids that were not feeling good, which unfortunately, is a typical situation for the middle of February. While we attended to the Mints that were feeling a little under the weather, Coaches announced for warm ups to be removed. The team headed off hand in hand, they seemed extremely confident as they walked off.

With Cheersport the pressure is turned up immensely. The coaches are always dialed in, but during Cheersport everything is turned up a notch. Most coaches are involved with three Stingray teams across the program. They have a ton on their minds and many scenarios running through their head. What they are confident about is the preparation their teams put into practicing routines. At this point in the season Peppermint could complete the routine in their sleep. It was just a matter of executing flawlessly. The team wanted to get off to a good start as the competition was always very strong at Cheersport. Mini Level 1 teams came from all over the nation to compete. This was also the first step to achieving their goal to win the Triple Crown.

My Team Dad duties were complete at this point. I am not going to lie; I get very emotional once Peppermint heads for the warm up room. My thoughts immediately shift to how incredibly proud I am of all these athletes. I keep trying to put myself in their position. Staring out and walking along close to 70,000 people that will converge on this competition at their age. Going out on that stage and executing perfection every single time is the goal but it has to be very intimidating. To this point, there has not been a chink in the armor. As I am thinking about Peppermint, the large parents group walks toward the arena to grab our seats and we part ways to watch my other daughter compete with the Grape Rays. I stop and smirk and think how four and five year olds do the same thing. It is simply amazing.

Grape opened up the Cheersport with a fantastic performance and a "Hit". As nervous as I get during competitions, I am always relieved a bit when the Grape Rays go out and do their thing and hit. They are so fun to watch and when they do well it helps with my nerves. We headed toward the hall Peppermint was performing at. As we were waiting in the parent viewing area, I noticed the crowd forming to watch Peppermint. We saw a huge support network from all the other Stingray families. I noticed a large portion of Black Warm Up outfits emerge and there they were again, The Orange Rays and Peach Rays and many other Stingrays teams making their way to watch Peppermint. Words cannot describe the feeling when the teams you look up to at Stingrays, come to support your Mini Level 1 team.

As the coaches made their way to the front of the stage, the mad dash began to get to the preferred viewing area to watch our team. As I mentioned, we are a very superstitious group. When the team takes the stage most of the athletes will look for their parents in a specific spot. It is a small thing but very soothing for them to know that you are there in the same spot every time.

Once I got in my position I noticed the prayer circle for the coaches was much larger. Normally it is our four coaches, this time there was seven. A few of the coaches from other teams came over to support the Mints as they were about to hit the stage. It was such an incredible gesture and as the team ran out on the stage amongst the flashing lights of the Cheersport stage. The team noticed the extra entourage of coaches. They all smiled as they could see everyone. It made them feel special and it was about to be go time.

As the team readied for their performance you could see them focusing and getting ready. As Coach Ashley gave the thumbs up to start the music, my stomach dropped. The signature music started with a loud "Welcome to Mintland the greatest place on earth has blue and green turf. It's always a magical day when you're a MINT RAY." The team was off and the facials were coming fast and furious. This team was fired up and ready to deliver. The routine progressed toward the "stunt of death" and I looked over to some of the coaches who were from out of town and have never watched Peppermint before. They were caught off guard by the precision of the stunt and you could tell they were impressed by their smiles. The team went on to an even better pyramid and the dance was astounding. At the end of the routine the team knew they nailed it. Peppermint bolted off the stage and they were ecstatic! The crowd was buzzing from the performance.

As we were walking out of the viewing area I overheard a parent from another gym say "Wow that was a Mini team?" It was a very nice gesture from the gym and it showed great sportsmanship.

As the team gathered to be released to their parents Coach Ashley did an amazing job speaking with the team. One of the most important life lessons she teaches her teams is to remain very humble and focused. She reminds the team that they have to work on a few things in the routine and that this is a two day competition. One day does not make a National Championship. She wrapped up her speech and asked the team if they had any questions. One of the Mints asked if they did even better on Sunday could the team get "Dippin Dots." Coach Ashley looked over at me smiled and asked if I could help make that happen, I said absolutely! The team roared with excitement with the challenge that was before them. The gauntlet was thrown down. Dippin dots were now on the line.

The team scurried off in their separate ways. Some to watch and encourage family members or friends on other Stingray teams competing. Some went off to meet with friends from around the country that they have made at other competitions. Some went home to unwind and relax for Day 2 of the competition. After about an hour, I started receiving text from the parents. "How do you think we did?" "When are we going to hear what place we are in after Day one?" "Have you heard from Ashley yet?"

I loved our parent group. The entire group was so excited for this team and every parent knew how to get the most out of their child and get them to work together. I was excited to find out myself. With a competition this large it would take a few hours to find out the results for Day one. I would take this opportunity to have some fun with the parents to keep the mood light. I would respond, "Yes I have the results but I have been told not to share them" when I really did not have the results. Silly things like that to keep the mood light. We watched some incredible teams at Cheersport in the mini level one division. It was going to be close if we were to be at the top for day one.

Later that afternoon I received a text from Coach Ashley. She was very excited. Peppermint was in 1st Place after day one. They were one step closer to completing their first challenge of winning Cheersport. After reading the text, I looked over to my wife and gave her a nod that I had some results. I did not want to break the news to my daughter until the time was right. I also had to think of the perfect way to share with the parents. Sharing information to the team is always critical. I know all the parents were waiting on pins and needles waiting to hear from me. I also had the added element of my younger daughter in play here. I was always cautious to make sure I was equally excited no matter where my daughter's team placed after day one. It was always easy if both teams were in first place. It is a very delicate situation if the teams are anywhere other than first place. Or worse, one is ahead of the other. My daughters watch our reaction very closely and they both want equal reassurance from us. I was hoping to receive news from my younger daughters' team momentarily. After a few minutes we got the text. The Grape Rays were also in first place but just by a small amount. We would leave out that part when sharing the information with my daughters. As we normally do, we go to get lunch and I begin to craft the text out to the Peppermint parents. After I craft the text, we share the good news with my daughters. They immediately begin decompress as they hear the good news. The tension is lifted off, if for only a few hours. They enjoy their lunch and start to enjoy the moment for a few hours. They have both been here before, and they know what to do.

Just a few minutes later all of the texts start pouring in from the Peppermint parents. Of course, they are ecstatic. Everyone then shifts their focus to twitter as the news from the other Stingray teams starts to pour in. People feverishly refreshing their phones glued to @CheerUpdates looking for the hieroglyphic code that only dedicated cheer parents can understand. Everyone looks for that elusive three letter word from @CheerUpdates that is only given when earned, all teams yearn for their team name to be followed by a "HIT" after they perform. It is a nod from a very well respected critic in the cheer world.

As day one winds down. I craft a text message to the parents reminding them of the agenda for the following morning and also reminding them of the importance of a good night sleep. Keeping the team in good spirits and well rested is a huge advantage heading into day 2. Morning arrives and we load up the vehicle for day two. To my delight, there were no texts this morning involving sick children or people running late. My prayers were answered and the team has a relatively stress free trip into the competition. As the team arrives at Cheersport the team is in great spirits. All of the parents begin to make eye contact with each other to make sure they are truly ok. As a cheer parent you need to be good at hiding any drama that may be lurking behind the scenes. I have seen it happen all too often. A forgotten bow, skirt, uniform or shoes can spell nightmare. As Team Dad, I have to have it all covered. Extra lip stick, band aids, extra bows, shoe laces, socks, nail polish remover, cotton swabs, pepto bismol, and childrens aspirin anything you could think of I had loaded down in my Nfinity backpack ready for that look of desperation from a parent or coach.

Luckily, this morning it was just a few magic tummy pills for nervous Peppermints. On day two for large competitions the vibe is a little different. Some of the team is loose and are playing. Most of the others like to stay quiet and relax. I would like to think they are focused on their routine, but these are six, seven, and eight year old kids, so who knows what they are thinking about. At such a young age they know what is on the line. They have been coached well. It is about doing their best and focusing. They know they will need to come out with a ton of energy to impress the judges. All they really want to do is make Coach Ashley happy with their effort. As I scan the room, I make eye contact with Beecher. He was playing in the hallway I walk over to him and he looks up at me and asks, "Do you think we will do well today?" I looked back at him and said "I know you are going to be fantastic" He smiled back. A few minutes later we heard the announcement for warm ups off. It was time for Day two. The team joined hands and headed toward warm ups. The Stingray parent contingency cheered as Peppermint headed down the hallway.

My heart sank with nerves, but I was confident in the team's ability to get it done. The parents all headed toward the arena. As all the mini teams began to perform they all took it to the next level. Day two scoring is different than day one and things can change dramatically with a bobble here or a fall there. You need to "Hit" on both days to be considered in the top three. As the parents all watch the rest of the competing teams many eyebrows were raised at the level of competition this year. These teams were good. Peppermint was going to need their A game today.

As the last team completed their routine it was time for Peppermint. I was shocked by the swarms of people coming into the VIP viewing area to watch our Mints. We had a huge contingency from

Stingrays following us up to the stage. The crowd carefully allowing the parents of the team to get their "spot" and then everyone else quickly fills in around them. It was easy to get very emotional at the outpouring of support that was happening.

As the coaches made their way from behind the stage, there was a large coach's entourage that followed. Many of the other Stingray coaches again came out in support to watch Peppermint. I noticed Coach Ashley confidently came out from behind the stage. I made eye contact with Coach Ashley and she gave me a quick nod. She knew what I was going to ask her if I had the chance. I would always ask her how the team looked. She took pity on me by giving me a little nod.

The team came out on the stage and each of the minis made eye contact with their respective parents and then proceeded to get mentally prepared for the music to start. They seemed focused and confident. A few of the coaches were slamming the mat to get the attention of a few that were lined up a little off. This had to be perfect. A split second of eerie silence falls on the arena. Everyone's eyes turn to Coach Ashley waiting for her to give the thumbs up to cue the music. All of this seems like an eternity as a parent, and then the music blares. Welcome to Mint Land… and then they were off.

Day two to me is always a blur. At this stage of the year, I know the routine like the back of my hand. I can also tell the vibe of the team after a few seconds. As I scan the entire mat, I like what I am seeing from the team. The energy is electric and the team looks like they are having a blast. The execution is flawless and the confidence is beaming. The stunt of death left the crowd stunned and the pyramid lit up the stage. As the team started into the dance you could tell they knew they were close to being done and the excitement took them to the next level. The team was beaming as Beecher began his iconic roll that was set to the "I just can't wait to be King" music from "The Lion King." At the end of the routine Beecher hit the final pose with his beaming smile. The crowd erupts with cheering and applause. I looked over to my wife, smiled and said I think they "Hit" again!

As you leave the performance all of the parents confer to make sure everyone saw the same thing. In a live competition there is so much to see and everything is going so fast it is easy to miss a bobble or a fall. After talking to most everyone we all agreed Peppermint "Hit" on Day two. Of course this was a consensus from the parents. The judges may have another perspective on the performance. We needed to wait and see.

As we waited for the team to emerge from behind the stage, the parent's area was buzzing. We were all very optimistic about the team's chances. I walked back behind the screen and the Peppermints were watching a replay of their performance as a team. As the final seconds of the dance wrapped up I could see the team jumping up and down as they were excited with the performance. Coach Ashley said they did a great job and did they best they could. They all starting jumping up and down as the words of admiration from the coach they have learned to respect so much meant the world to them. Then with a surmounting energy you knew what the next question was going to be. One of the more spunky Peppermints started with a coy looking face and began to speak. "So... Coach Ashley... since we did our best, yesterday you mentioned we might be able to get Dippin Dots if we did our best today." The team erupted in jeering and screams asking if they won their Dippin Dots. Coach Ashley looked over at me and said "I think they may have earned them do you think so?" I nodded in approval and the entire team erupted in cheers. Many of the Peppermint began doing their happy dance. As many cheer parents know. Many of the world's problems can be solved with a healthy helping of Dippin Dots. The team was excited and they ran toward the vendor to redeem their prize.

Team Waiting for their Dippin Dots after Day 2 Cheersport

We started making our way back to the award ceremony. Normally there are a few hours between the competition and the awards ceremony. Since Cheersport is such a large competition they have to compress the awards ceremonies and we had a shorter window of time. The awards began in about 45 minutes which seems like a long time but while walking back, it seemed like we were rushing. The Georgia World Congress center feels like you are walking literally for miles to get from one end to the next. It is a long walk, not to mention you are weaving in-between thousands of team's parents and athletes on the way back.

Coach Ashley informed me I needed to remain with the team after awards as she had to get her final team ready for competition and Coach Kelsey and Jessica were going to be performing. As the team assembled for awards, I headed toward the back of the group. There waiting for me, as always, was my buddy Beecher. This time it was a little different for Beecher as the size and scope of this competition was a bit much for adults to take in much less young children. Cheersport is huge, couple that with thousands of people and chaos and it can be a bit intimidating for children. Beecher took my hand and we started to head out for the award ceremony. Since this was Beecher's first very large competition he had quite a few questions for me. "Mr. Eric are all these people here to see our awards ceremony?" I said well Beech they are all here to see all of the teams that have competed today. You guys competed against a bunch of great teams."

He said ok. "There sure are a bunch of people out there." I said "Yup but a lot of the people are all mommies and daddies of the teams you competed against along with brother and sisters Grandmas and Grandpas." Beecher then began to talk about his sisters teams. "I really wish my sisters teams do well; I really want them to do well." I could tell Beech was a little nervous with the entire situation. I changed the subject to a topic I knew would make him feel more comfortable. I asked him what kind of Dippin Dots he got. His face lit up and we carried on our conversation until they were instructed to file onto the stage for awards.

What struck me as odd was the whole time I was with Peppermint, not one of them asked me if they thought they would win. They were just satisfied with doing their best and that was all that mattered to them. The awards ceremony began and the tension mounted. As the MC was announcing the finishing position I noticed the team locked arms in unison as a team. With each team name that was announced, Peppermint squeezed tighter and tighter. I can only imagine what is going in their little heads as I scan the entire arena from the back of the awards stage. The final few teams are left to be announced and Peppermint is visibly emotional. They are hunched over together with locked arms as a group. The MC announces the second place team and Peppermint stays composed as a team in unison to honor the second place team who has worked just as hard all year. Peppermint gives the team a round of applause and cheers for them. As the second place team makes their way off the stage the MC announces. "Your 2015 Cheersport National Champions the Stingray Allstars Peppermint!"

The team went berserk and the crowd gave the team a standing ovation. Peppermint went up to gather their hardware which was a huge banner for the gym and a trophy. As the team left the stage it was time for the team to gather in the Champions area to be fitted for their National Championship jackets and for me to distribute medals to the team.

The Coaches had a few minutes to celebrate with the team and they really made the team feel special. Together we helped gather all the correct jacket sizes for the team. We waited patiently as a team while all the other National Champions from other divisions had their time in front of the photographer to complete team photos. We watched as the MC announced the team as National Champions to the awaiting parents, grandparents and friends waiting in the Champions area. The kids were excited and were asking me if they got to go up on stage and do that too. I smiled and said, "You sure do!"

The team proceeded to go out on the big stage to take group pictures with their National Championship Banner and Trophy. Their faces said it all when they walked out as a group. The photographers lined them up and they all wanted their picture taken with the big trophy. They were equally as excited to take a group picture with their big sisters behind the scenes. It was a very special day for all of them as Peach went on to become Cheersport National Champions later that day.

Peppermint 2015 Cheersport National Champions

9 NCA

The day following competitions is next to unbearable for most families. Cheersport being one of the biggest and mentally taxing did not help the situation any. If you have been around the sport you will hear the term "Cheer Hangover" it refers to the feeling of mental and physical exhaustion after completing two days of competition. It is real, and it is tough to function the day after a competition. What surprises me to no end is that the gym is absolutely packed the day after a competition. The teams get back to the gym to work on tumbling skills, body positions, stunts etc. Both of my daughters went to tumble and we saw most of the Peppermints in the gym sporting their new jackets. It was time to get back to work. NCA was coming up next and that competition was going to be a huge challenge.

NCA would be the second leg of the Triple Crown and is always the toughest competition for many reasons. The competition at NCA is second to none. It is hands down the deepest pool of talent at any competition. The Mini Level 1 division would be no exception. The NCA jacket is the most coveted prize for an All Star Cheerleader. NCA is rich with history and tradition. The competition is very well run and it is a very prestigious event. If you leave with an NCA jacket you wear it with pride for as many years as you can. Peppermint won NCA the previous year but it would be tough to repeat the performance.

Peppermint only had a week and a half to prepare. The gym was electric with intensity and focus. The Mints get extremely excited for this competition as they get to go on an airplane. It's a really big deal for the kids and they get very excited. Logistically speaking NCA is a huge challenge to get everyone in Dallas in one piece. With delayed flights, unpredictable weather, busses and rental cars the travel can be overwhelming. All has to go perfect to get the entire gym in the building ready to go.

As practiced pushed on, the relationship with their big sisters Peach grew immensely. Peach won Cheersport as well, and they had big aspirations to finish off the season strong. Peach continued to make Peppermint feel like rock stars in the gym as they continued to cheer them on at practice. There could not be better mentors for Peppermint. Peach came early and stayed late to perfect their routine every practice. They practiced with a smile on their face the entire time. They were focused on being the best and the coaches expected nothing less. The bond of Peach was mirrored on a smaller scale with Peppermint. They both had hearts of Champions built upon the camaraderie and bond of the team. With a strong week of practice the team was ready to head to Dallas.

The parents organized a fun sendoff party for the Mints before they left for Dallas. It was a great way to get the team pumped up for the competition. The team was excited as we got them a cookie cake that incorporated the iconic "I got 99 problems but a Peach aint one." which was the voice over from the now famous Peach Rays music. It was a great idea from one of the parents. The parents wanted to personalize the cake and we changed the "Peach" to "Mint". So the cake read "I got 99 problems but a Mint aint one." It represented the bond between the two teams and Peppermint was ecstatic. It was a nice touch and was a great way to make the team feel great.

NCA Send Off Celebration Cake

It was time to head out toward Dallas which meant a Stingray take over at the Atlanta Hartsfield Airport. As the teams made their way toward Dallas all the parents were glued to weather report as the reports were not good. It was supposed to snow the entire weekend. Parents, who were already stressed, now had to deal with potential weather delays and cancelled flights. It was not a fun time to be a cheer parent. An overly stressed parent rubs off on a cheerleader. Grumpy mini cheerleaders are not a good way to start one of the most important competitions of the year. The good news was that everyone made it to their hotels at a decent hour and this year the tiny and mini teams competed later on in the day on

Friday instead of Saturday early morning. The bad news was, it began to snow early afternoon on Friday and we had to fight rush hour traffic to get down to the convention center. I also received word we had an extremely sick Peppermint and we were not sure she was going to be able to compete.

Once I got word of our sick Mint, I immediately contact Coach Ashley as she would need to potentially think of a plan B. Needless to say, it was not a very good beginning to our NCA trip. The busses were running extremely late and parents were starting to panic as they were not sure they were going to be able to make the meet time for the team. The good news was that the entire team was going to be late as we were all in the same boat. Logistically we were challenged and extremely stressed, but eventually everyone was accounted for on the busses. We had to make room for the teams and coaches and eventually all parents and teammates made it to the venue. My shoulder was used the entire 45 minute trip to prop up our sick Peppermint who was brave enough to make the trip down to the venue without her Mom. Due to logistical challenges the bus that took the team to the arena was packed full. We had to make a decision to have her Mom wait for the following busses as the team and coaches took first priority to be on busses. It was a tough situation and a very brave move. She was very sick, but did not want to miss the competition. We would need to monitor her situation and make a last minute call.

The stress level was intense as parents were trickling in from the bus ride. The snow was bad and getting worse. We were one of the first groups to make it to the arena and it was empty. Normally, the convention center is packed with thousands of athletes and spectators. The silence was an eerie feeling but the convention center was filling quickly. Peppermint headed toward the Stingray warm up room and it was full of Rays within 45 minutes. Teams were arriving fast and it was not the normal morning routine for our athletes. The team looked good in pre-warm up and our sick mint was looking a bit better. Her teammates were making sure she felt ok and they had her back. The adrenaline was starting to kick in for the entire team. They were getting into form and getting their game faces on. They knew the importance of this competition. As the team worked in a jam packed warm up room they looked ready to go. Peppermint headed toward warm ups and they lined up as they always do. With a loud roar from the parents they were off. The next time we would see them would be on stage.

As we watched the other teams compete in the hour before Peppermint went on, you could tell the competition was different. The tiny teams are extraordinary. All of them from top to bottom. The mini teams that went on early were spectacular. You could tell this was going to be a huge battle for Peppermint.

At NCA the competition is set up differently than most. The viewing area for the parents that is typically right in front of the stage is moved off to the left. They do not allow anyone but coaches in front. The competition does not want anything to be taken away from the performance on stage. The competition does an incredible job focusing the attention on the athletes. The blessing and the curse of NCA is that it is all about the athletes being alone by themselves as a team and being one with the routine and their coach. From the moment you walk in until awards the environment is consistent.

The change in the viewing area created a bit of a challenge in my mind. I stated earlier we were a very superstitious bunch and consistency and routine was very important to all of us. The team not being able to make eye contact with us before they started worried me. The team not feeling the energy from the viewing area from those screaming them on worried me. The Tiny, Mini, and Youth teams performed on a different day than the rest of the older teams. We would not have our normal entourage of the Stingray Nation with us. All of this was weighing on my mind.

As we were getting closer to the performance time for Peppermint the Mini Level 1 teams were performing and they were good. One after the other completed their routines and more often than not they were flawless. A few had some challenges or small bobbles but you could tell the competition was on top of their game. Peppermint had to nail it with the attitude they normally bring.

Being the team dad, I felt the parent's eyes piercing into my soul as I was not back with the team on this competition. I knew it was in my mind, but I felt that parents were looking for a sign from me. I was sitting in the arena like everyone else, but felt helpless as I had no idea how the team was looking or feeling. I kept checking my phone every ten seconds making sure I did not miss a message from Coach Ashley. I wanted to make sure our sick athlete did not need something. In reality, I think I was just looking to get a piece of assurance to pass onto everyone. I was hoping by some miracle I could go back to watch the team warm up and I knew after watching them for less than fifteen seconds I could tell how they were going to do. As a team dad, I did not want to let anyone down. I was clearly thinking too much and before I knew it, Peppermint was on deck.

At NCA it is very challenging to sit together as a parents group. We tried as best we could to sit together to maximize the economies of scale that would be our voices on that day. As the team in front of Peppermint heads into their dance sequence, I knew it was time. My palms get sweaty and parents start making eye contact with each other as we know it is about time. With a simple capture of each other eyes we as a group know what that glance means. The parents were coming together like no group I have ever been associated with. Today, we were going to be loud and we would will our children out of an environment they are not used to being in. It was a long and stressful day for the parents in more ways than one, but now the focus turned to the stage.

As the previous team left the stage all of our eyes were scrambling to find our kids. We all wanted to capture a glimpse of their spirit. Were they ok, were they smiling, how was our sick Mint? As I scanned Coach Ashley for a sign, or a glimpse of what was about to come, unfortunately I could not get a good read, as she was focused on getting the team ready for their two minute and thirty second journey. I watched as parents desperately try to capture their child's attention, if for only one second to make sure that they knew they were there. Once all of that was complete, all eyes turned toward the middle of the stage as we wait for Coach Ashley to give the thumbs up. I smirk to myself as I think about the goal of the NCA competition set up. As hard as we tried to make the environment as familiar as possible, the competition won on this day. It was all up to the team, the coach, the routine they know and nothing more. It is pure competition in its truest and cleanest form.

After what seems like an eternity, I open my eyes after a deep breath and see the thumbs up. The team ignites with anticipation and then a thunderous sound of the music beginning and the powerful voiceover "Welcome to MintLand" begins. The team erupts as the adrenaline of the moment takes over. I quickly scan over to our sick Mint. She seems ok, but not the spunky smiling fireplug she normally is. The routine began strong as they prepared for the opening. The team was building momentum. The timing was perfect as they launched into formation for "stunt of death". The sequence went off without a hitch. They transitioned into their pyramid and my knees went weak for a split second, which is normal after the tension releases from watching the stunt. The pyramid was flawless and they were almost home. As the team entered into the dance, the energy level was amazing the tension was being emitted from the screams of parents cheering this team on. Through sickness, travel drama and an uncomfortable environment they did it. Peppermint hit on Day 1.

As the team left the stage, the parents hurried over to meet the team. While were walking over as a group we were met with a huge sea of humanity that was entering the arena. It seemed another gym that was about to compete, brought a huge entourage of supporters with them. The parents all milled about and were ecstatic about Peppermints performance. We were all relieved and so proud of this team and their consistency. Coach Ashley and the team were watching the performance as a group and shared sound advice to make a great performance even better for tomorrow. As the team was released, the kids were desperately looking for their parents to get huge hugs and support from the ones they love. As we as a group distribute the accolades they deserve, I begin to drift out back towards the front of the stage to watch the final mini team perform. My oldest daughter slowly follows me out as she began to realize I was watching the final team in their division perform.

As I began to focus on the team on stage I noticed the huge entourage of people lining the viewing area on the left side of the stage. It was a very impressive group and they were very loud and encouraging. The team music started and they were very clean out of the gate. The routine progressed and they just kept building momentum. As I watched the entire routine the arena was electric with energy. The California Allstars brought a huge following and the routine was absolutely flawless. My daughter turned around, looked at me raised her eyebrows and said, "Wow they were really, really good. " I responded yes they were, "but you can get um."

As my daughter smiled and turned to make our way back to the bus for the hotel my heart sank, I just witnessed an incredible performance that threatened our teams winning streak. I tried to come off as confident, but humble in front of my daughter. I did not want her to think I did not believe in her or her team. Maybe I was just stressed and tired. Maybe I was overthinking how good the California mini team was. I looked over at my wife and she gave me a look I feared. I looked for a second opinion from the sea of parents making their way out of the arena. I found one of the many trusted experienced cheer parents. The second we made I contact, I knew. She saw what I saw.

As Parents it is our job to keep our Peppermints energized and pumped up about their incredible performance. Our kids know us better than we know ourselves sometimes. The challenge to come off as business as usual was of the most importance. We would all make our way back to the hotel and await the scores from the judges from day one.

Waiting for the scores from Day one was one of the most difficult few hours of my life. Wanting to find out where we were while trying to keep my daughters in top spirits was a challenge. Habitually checking my phone every 10 seconds was getting exhausting. Text messages from the parents were coming in hot and heavy. They needed to know as badly as I did. More to prepare their kids for what they were about to face. I was confident this team could overcome anything. Then another text message alert came for me. It was not from a parent, it was from Coach Ashley. As I went to go read the text my knees went weak again. I read the message and my heart started to race. I scanned the message over five times to make sure I had all the information correct. As I had feared, we were in second place. As I process the information before me, my thoughts immediately shift to my daughters. I look over at my wife as she makes eye contact with me. When my daughters were not looking at me I quickly throw up two fingers to my wife indicating we are in second place. She gives me a nod. I then turn to my daughter. As my heart pounds with the anticipation of her reaction, I share the news that Peppermint is in second place after Day one. I am careful to share the news in an upbeat fashion so as not to seem that we as a family have lost faith in the team. She looks right back at me and said, "Ok, not to worry. Coach Ashley said that no matter where we placed on Day one we would come out much stronger on day two anyway so I'm not worried. Can we go to dinner know? I want to meet up with my friends."

I was floored. She did not even flinch. This is a life lesson that was taught to me by my daughter. It showed maturity, it showed confidence, and it was a reaction that was a reflection of the code that Peppermint lived by. "Do your best and that is all that I expect of you." This was a reflection of the coaching this team was provided with from the top down.

At that point it hit me. I should not be worrying about the team's confidence. The biggest challenge for me would be to keep the parents spirits up. As I prepared to share the news with the entire Peppermint team via text message, I struggle with how to present the news. After over thinking the entire message, I forward a lightly edited version of what Coach Ashley sent me out to the group. We headed out as a family to meet friends for dinner and then it began. As I suspected, the text replies begin to overflow my phone. Worried parents are struggling with the news. Some of the parents are new this year and are looking for guidance on what they can do differently. I know I am not going to be able to touch each one of the parents to calm them all. The kids were fine the team was confident the coaches were confident. The only way I knew I could help as a team dad was to subliminally change the spirits of the parents. Then it hit me, much to the dismay of my wife I spent thirty to forty five minutes crafting out a group of messages on Twitter that would hopefully get the parents back into good spirits. I know the parents are all glued to twitter watching Cheer Updates to find out how the other Stingray teams are doing. Then I sent the first tweet out waited a few minutes until the first retweet notice came from the tweet. One of the parents saw the tweet and got the message. The tweet was centered on the essence of this team. It was a picture of a previous competition that captured their spirit and attitude. I sent out enough tweets until I felt the parents got the message. This team had never let us down and it was not going to happen at this competition either. The tweets were scheduled to go out every thirty minutes. I began to get a few messages that confirmed the parents were getting the theme of the tweets. Kids were going to bed early and it was going to be ok no matter what happened the following day.

The following day the team began to assemble. Travel to the venue went much smoother on day two. The stress level was a bit lower and you could tell Peppermint was very loose and relaxed. Our sick Mint felt much better compared to the day before and you could tell she had her spunkiness back. The team seemed fired up. They have never had their backs to the wall before, but these young kids seemed to thrive under pressure. You could tell they had a chip on their shoulder as they had never been in second place after day one. Not that any of that mattered to them. They never knew the difference. All that mattered to them was doing their best. That is all that Coach Ashley had ever asked of them.

As they inched closer heading out to warm ups the leaders of the team began to emerge and started to get the team fired up. In their own way, they knew how to get the most out of each teammate. They would simulate the routine with their dolls that they bring to the competition. They would pump each other up and tell each other they need to bring that Peppermint attitude today. It was really remarkable to watch. You could tell they had been influenced by the older girls in the gym. They watch the older girls every move and model them to no end. Luckily for us, we have some of the most incredible role models in the world.

Peppermint was in second place by over a point which does not sound like a lot, but in competitive cheer it is a pretty wide margin. We would need a flawless routine and a little luck from the judges to take it over the top. The parents kept telling their children the same thing over and over. "Just do the best you can do." That is all we ask. I could tell the team had a gleam in their eye and an attitude about them. They wanted this bad, and we were excited for the team.

Honestly, at this point as parents we knew the team had nothing to lose. They have already had such an incredible season. The triple-crown was a goal that they wanted, but if it were not to happen they could easily walk away from the season incredibly proud. They were not thinking about that right now. They had one thing in mind and that was to show that they were the best Mini team in the world just like Coach Ashley said they could be.

Coach Kelsey gave the signal to take warm ups off. It was time, and they were pumped. The heart and soul of this team was when they were all together mentally. You could see with their sick teammate feeling better, they knew it was going to be special. The team held hands in pairs and was ready to make their way to warm ups. The crowd cheered as they always did. Beecher was in the back as he always is, escorting the team to their destination. As Peppermint makes their way down the hall Beecher and I make eye contact. I give him thumbs up; he returns the thumbs up with a smile. They were off and in great spirits.

The parents started to make their way to the arena. The walk is a long slow walk as we discuss the different scenarios that could potentially play out. The parents did their job. All of the team made it in one piece and they were in a great mood. Parents always want to do more, but at this stage in the game it is out of our hands. We discuss seating strategy and send out numerous tweets in hopes that our Stingray nation will come to cheer on our Peppermints. We know they will, and we can't wait for their arrival. The entire Stingrays family was now present in Dallas as many of the older teams first day of competition started today. We would have a better chance with the heart and soul of our gym cheering us on as well. We were going to need every advantage we could get to make it over the top.

On day two the teams compete in reverse order of standings. So we would go second to last and then The California Allstars would be the last team to compete in the division. As we watched the rest of the teams compete, the day two stresses could be felt throughout the arena. The tiny and mini team impress so many, as they get up on that stage in front of hundreds, if not thousands of people and do their thing. As it gets closer to ShowTime for Peppermint, I am unable to sit still. I begin to walk around the arena in hopes that my nerves will settle. They do not. I am habitually looking at my phone making sure I do not miss any messages from Coach Ashley, knowing that the last thing she would be doing is texting me about something. She is dialed into the team right now making sure that they are prepared to do their best. I am scanning the arena looking for Peppermint parents who are still looking to get closer to the stage and closer to the rest of the other parents. The arena is jam packed and no one is moving. I make eye contact with a few parents they give me a little smile and a nod as we know we are both going through the same emotions.

As the announcement is made that Peppermint is on deck, last minute deals are struck with parents viewing other teams to beg and plead to get a seat a few feet closer to the stage. Promising just to watch their child and then surrender the seat back. I look up and notice the sea of green T-Shirts entering the arena coupled with an army of Black, Blue and White warm up uniforms. It's the Stingray family entourage coming to cheer our Peppermints on and we are rolling deep. The Stingray families just kept flowing into the arena it was a huge relief to see that support coming to cheer your team on. The emotions are truly indescribable. With the rush of excitement and confidence that our cheering section was in place. I began scanning backstage for our Peppermints. My wife and I positioned ourselves best we could to make sure the team knew we were there. On this day we had an army of support to make noise. Now it was up to the team and the coaches to make it happen. When the MC announced the team onto the stage, the coaching staff made their way out in front. The team came out with a look I have yet to see. They were pumped, mad, excited, determined and confident all at once.

Coach Ashley slaps the mat to get a few of the Peppermints perfectly aligned. Once everyone is in place she gives them a small smile and gives the thumbs up. The music starts and the team erupts into action. After watching the team for about fifteen seconds I look over to my wife, smile and say "They're back." I could tell instantly this was going to be an incredible performance. It is magical to watch young kids perform in the zone. The stunts were flawless, the heel stretches and scale were all gorgeous. The jumps were all perfectly synchronized which led to the pyramid that was capped off with an emphatic group of confident smiles. The momentum led them into the final dance of the NCA competition and the crowd roared and all clapped in perfect unison to the beat of the Peppermint music. As Beecher made his final forward roll into the center of the stage and lit up the crowd with his electric smile it was over.

Peppermint made it look effortless. Once the music stopped, they all looked at each other in amazement. They knew they had done it, a hit on day two at NCA with their backs against the wall. As a parent, I could not have been more proud. Coach Ashley was ecstatic and glowing with emotion. They left it all out on the floor. The team bolted off stage into the welcoming arms of their coaches. As they cried tears of joy the team huddled together to watch the magnificent performance once again on the monitor. The parents were buzzing and elated. All the parents agreed the team did all they could do. We all awaited the arrival of the team. As the Mints all hustled to find their parents I catch my daughter running to me. At full speed she runs into my arms crying with excitement. It was an incredible moment. We all hugged as a family and congratulated her for a great performance.

A few moments later it hit us. The final team needed to perform.

Coach Ashley informs me she will not be able to watch the final team as she had to prepare her other team for competition. She needed me to escort the team to awards and stay with the team. She would be back in time to make it on stage for the award ceremony. She wanted me to text her how the California Allstars did. Cali was about to hit the stage. I noticed they did not have as big of an entourage as they did the previous day. That made sense, as the older teams would be preparing to compete on this day. The team music started and they came out strong. As our entire family watched the team perform, I wanted to remain as unbiased as I could. It is easy to show favoritism and allegiance to your gym. It is how you are programmed. I wanted to be able to tell my daughter honestly when the inevitable question was asked. I knew the "Daddy do you think we could win?" Question was coming. I wanted to be prepared to give an honest and direct response.

As I scanned the entire stage looking for anything out of the ordinary, nothing seemed out of place, they looked good so far. The pyramid section was coming up and the tension was mounting. As the team completed their pyramid there may have been a small bobble. I saw it, but it was very minor. My daughters who were incredible students of the sport, both immediately looked back at me as they saw the same thing. I saw them look at me out of the corner of my eye, but I remained focused on watching the rest of the performance as to not miss anything. They were waiting for a reaction from me. Out of sheer respect for the sport, in no way shape or form was I going to give them one. As a parent and as a team representative you never celebrate the misfortunes of another team no matter how big or small. At that moment, the most important thing to me was that my daughters saw that I did not respond to that bobble.

California Allstars finished the routine very strong. My daughters both looked up at me and my oldest tugged on my jeans and asked. "Daddy how do you think they did?" I responded, "Honey, they looked incredible, but so did you guys. It's too close to call at this point" I sent over the text to Ashley and told her what I saw. The scoring is a bit different on day two compared to day one so it would be in the judge's hands and it could be very close.

The Peppermints started to gather for awards and they were in great spirits. Many had snuck over to the Dippin Dots vendor to get a little treat before awards. We all gathered and I did a quick head count to make sure all Mints were accounted for. As always, they joined hands as a team and made their way behind the curtain to wait for awards. My buddy Beecher waited for me to join him in the back and we were off. As we were instructed by the security team, we found our spot to sit and wait. We were early and keeping eighteen kids busy and out of mischief was going to be a big challenge. Luckily another team arrived and as always, the Peppermints made new friends very quickly. Many of the team introduced themselves to one another and were just having fun being kids. They shared experiences and stories about their team and experiences. The other team began to ask about The Stingray Allstars Orange as well as Peach. The Mints welled with pride as they were able to share that they practice alongside both of the teams regularly. The also played a quick game of the "Telephone Game" which was a huge favorite with the group when we had some down time. The entire team made sure everyone was included and no one was left out. They did it instinctively, and it was inspiring to watch. They made a point to include the neighboring team as well.

It was truly special to see the sportsmanship and comradery of these teams up-close and personal. After a short visit, the team we were visiting with was moved to another part of the venue. I then began to get pelted with questions about the competition. I quickly diverted and focused back on the teams effort and stressed that they did their best and "Hit" on both days deduction free. The question was then posed to me. "Well did California Allstars Hit on both days as well?" I responded, "Yes, they sure did." Then it hit me like a ton of bricks. No matter what happened with the results, one of the teams on that awards stage was going to have to go through one of the toughest scenarios in Cheer. The scenario is explaining to your team that you "Hit" on both days but ended up coming in any place but first. At this young age, it is tough for teams to comprehend. It just does not register with them. I prayed that whatever happened on the awards stage the teams would learn valuable life lessons and build off this experience as many teams had "hit" on both days.

Just as the next question was about to be asked, Coach Ashley arrived just in time to escort the team up to the awards ceremony. I was excited and nervous all at the same time. Coach Ashley thanked me and dismissed me to return to the front of the stage to wait for the team after awards. The team waved and smiled as I wished them the best of luck. As the mini level 1 awards began, as always, I begin to get very nervous. The announcer began to announce the teams in reverse order. As he began to announce the top five, I began to think about the Peppermint goals, and what it meant to them. The team wanted to win the Triple Crown outright, which would mean winning each of the big three Cheersport, NCA and UCA. It was a lofty goal. With children this young the only thing that should matter is that they have fun, work hard as a team, and do the best they can do. That does not mean the team should not go for aggressive achievements.

There are two ways to win the Triple Crown, outright and by point standings. While winning by points was a huge achievement winning outright made a huge statement. Being a Mini team Peppermint was not eligible to earn a Summit bid as they were not old enough. The Triple Crown was the goal. They had pushed the limits of perfection all year. I was only hoping they could earn a spot at the top one more time.

As the MC began to announce the 4th place team you could see the tension on stage with the remaining teams. Each team began to lock arms with each other to support one another. With each team name called, it is a bittersweet moment for all involved as you watch teams walk up to receive their awards. All of the teams show incredible sportsmanship and respect for each other. With three teams remaining, I can see all the teams squinting eyes and silent prayers being muttered underneath their breath. Once another team is announced the remaining teams recoil from the tension and give the third place team a huge round of applause and cheer them on. Watching the sportsmanship on stage is truly inspiring as they give each other hugs of encouragement and waves of support.

It's down to the final two teams. The MC begins the NCA tradition of bringing both remaining coaches to the middle of the arena to shake hands and wish each other luck. As the announcer begins to look at the prepared document to announce the second place team, I focus on the kids. I drop my hands to my knees and bend over as my nervousness is hindering my ability to stand. The MC begins to speak, "And your second place finisher in the Mini Level 1 division. From Marietta, Georgia the Stingray Allstars Peppermint! My head shot up and immediately focused on the team. Some were excited, some were in shock, some were crying. They all stood up as a team as the rest of the teams surrounded them with cheers and applause. They made their way to receive the 2nd place banner. The California Allstars were announced the winning team and Peppermint and the coaches made sure to cheer them on as they were truly spectacular on this weekend.

Once all the teams were announced I knew what was about to happen. I headed over to the side of the stage to help escort the team off the platform. As expected many of the kids were extremely upset. Parents and Coaches were consoling the team. As every great leader does, Coach Ashley snapped into action. She called for one more team huddle before she dismissed the team. She roared with pride and made sure Peppermint knew how incredibly proud they made her. She reminded them that they did their very best and even though they were not the best team today. She was still emphatic when she told the team that she still knows that they are the best mini team in the world. She went on to tell the team to hold their heads high as they were true champions on this day. As the team broke, many of the kids crumbled into the arms of their parents. My daughter did the same as she just wanted a big hug and relief from the disappointment. They did not understand why they lost. It was an incredible opportunity to share another all so important life lesson. Sometimes in life, even though you do your very best, sometimes you will not be the victor. My youngest daughter's team hit their routine on both days as well, but finished fourth. As the parents share that life lesson in various ways, I take a moment to share how proud I am of my daughter's effort and sportsmanship. I emphasized how proud she should be of all her team accomplishments. As I began to run out of things to console her with, we as a family did what any smart parent would do in this situation. Offer up Dippin Dots to them. It was a rough competition for the entire Stingray gym. Many of the teams fell just short of becoming National Champions.

As we began walking down the long corridor back to the Stingray room, the taste of Dippin Dots soothed the agony of defeat just a bit. Many of the Mints were holding hands and were beginning to cheer up just a bit. One of our goals as a family was to see the famous arena at NCA. It is where many of the older teams perform and it is a magical place and visually stunning to see. I asked if my daughters wanted to go see. Unfortunately, they were both emotionally and physically exhausted. They were in no mood.

We began to head back to the bus and we sat together as a family along with most of our teammates. The team began to play together. Making sure no one was left out they began to make up cheer routines with the dolls they smuggled onto the bus. It was a long quiet ride back to the hotel. On the way to the airport the inevitable conversation came up. My oldest daughter brought up the Triple Crown. We as a family never really discussed the Triple Crown. She looked at me and said Daddy, "We can't win the Triple Crown now can we?" I looked at her and said, "You can still win the points race?" She responded, "What's the points race?" I begin to explain the rule of the triple-crown and how it all works with the three competitions. She seemed very excited as she began to understand how it all worked. She shared the exciting news with a few of the mints that were sitting on the bus with her. They seemed energized and excited. It was nice to be able to give them something to look forward to outside of doing their best at the next competition which was UCA. The parents began to discuss the possibilities. After winning Cheersport and placing second at NCA, Peppermint was in a great position to take home the Triple Crown championship by points total. The team would just have to have a good showing in the final competition and they could be in the running for the Triple Crown. It was time to head for the airport for the trek back to Marietta.

10 THE PEPPERMINT PLOT TWIST

The day after returning from Dallas, my daughters and I head to the gym for their tumble classes as usual. As we walked in, I could tell the gym did not have the normal energy. The competition took a lot out of everybody. It was a very stressful trip all the way around for all the teams. As I begin to look around, I see the usual suspects in the gym on the following day. Many of the Peppermints greeted each other and started tumbling and playing together. Many other athletes from other teams begin to file in as well. Parents were milling about and a few were chatting amongst themselves. I notice Coach Ashley walking briskly toward one of the parents from another team. She seemed overly energized talking with the parent. She saw me standing watching tumble class and came over to speak with me. She asked how the girls spirits were, I said they were both disappointed with the results but were in good spirits overall. I then asked, "How close was it?" Coach Ashley responded, "It was close." That was it. In true Stingrays fashion that would be all I got out of her. That was all I expected. I stated it would have been cool to win the Triple Crown outright, but we still had a great shot at winning the points race. I said we will be able to build that up as momentum to get the kids extra excited about competing at UCA.

After I said that Coach Ashley's face lit up. She seemed like she had something to tell me but was debating on whether or not she should. She responded, "Ok well about that, can you let the parents know we are going to have a mandatory meeting on Thursday night. I am going to need at least one parent represented for each athlete." I was a bit taken aback. I responded, "Ok what is the meeting about? Does this have anything to do with the Triple Crown?" She responded, "Well kind of, this should make up for this past weekend's results and that's all I can say at this point." I looked at her and said, "There is no way you can leave me hanging like that for four days." She looked at me and began to laugh as she was clearly bursting at the seams. She said, "Ok can you keep a secret until Thursday?" I said, "Sure."

Coach Ashley began to share her vision, "Ok so, you know the next competition is UCA. So what we are going to do is move Peppermint up an age group level and have them compete as a Youth Large team. I want to try to earn an "At Large" bid to enable them to compete at Summit. I think this team has the talent level to compete at the Youth level and do extremely well. I know it's a long shot, but I know this team can do it." My head and heart began racing. I did not know what to say. I had so many thoughts and questions in my mind but at this point I was so excited for this team, I honestly just wanted to burst into tears. The past weekend was tough pill to swallow for the team, but just the excitement of them getting the opportunity to try this would be a memory that would last a lifetime.

Coach Ashley then shared a few more details about how this masterplan would work. She did not waver one second. She knew this team had a great shot at executing and potentially winning an "at Large" bid. She just kept saying, "I know in my heart this team can do this, they have done it all year and this is what we are going to do." She asked me to not share any of this yet to others, as she did not have all the details buttoned up yet and would need until Thursday to share all the information with everyone. I agreed, but in my heart I had no idea how I was going to keep this incredible information a secret for over three days.

After tumble practice we put the kids to bed and I began drafting out the email to the Peppermint parents about the mandatory meeting. I knew once I sent this email out it was going to draw a bunch of questions from the parents. Speculation began almost immediately after the email was sent. Many guesses were made, but no one was even close to guessing what Coach Ashley was going to share with them. As some of the behind the scenes pieces fell into place it was quickly Thursday and it was almost time for practice.

Coach Ashley made sure all the parents were present. She shut the door behind her and set the stage for the news. Ashley thanked all of the parents for the incredible support they have provided up to this point. She shared how she was very proud of the team, and what they have accomplished so far this year. She also acknowledged that this past weekend was a tough loss for the team. Coach Ashley then paused. She then said, "I think there is a way to cheer the team up, and get them focused for the next challenge which is UCA."

One of the parents asked about the purpose of the mandatory meeting and why we needed one parent for each athlete represented. Coach Ashley took a deep breath and responded, "Well I am glad you asked, the reason I called this meeting is that after consulting with the coaching staff here at Stingrays, I want to make Peppermint a Youth Large team and have them compete at UCA." As I looked around the room some of the parents knew what that meant, some did not. One of the parents asked, "So our Mini team would be competing against Youth teams that are nine, ten, and eleven years old." Coach Ashley responded, "Yes that is correct, we want to do this in an attempt to win an "at large" bid to compete at Summit at the ESPN Wide World of Sports in Orlando. I know this was not on anyone's radar as of course Mini teams are not eligible to compete at Summit." This would also come with a few stipulations as we could not take a bid from another Stingray team who has not yet won a Summit bid." "I also need everyone to understand there could potentially be some additional costs involved if we should earn an "at large" bid to summit and I need to make sure everyone is on board with this decision before we proceed." Coach Ashley explained all of the different scenarios and how they would play out to all of the parents. Another parent then asked, "Have you informed the team about this?" Ashley responded, "No, I wanted to let you know first to make sure everyone is ok with it, and then I was going to tell the team at the beginning of practice tonight." Then the question was asked, "Can we watch you tell them?" Coach Ashley smiled and said, "Absolutely."

All of the parents filed out and headed toward to window that overlooked the gym. You could see the team frolicking on the mat like they normally do. Coach Ashley motioned the team to gather around. All of the coaches surrounded the team and began to explain the vision. While standing up in the parents viewing area, word quickly started to spread. A few parents from other teams began to wander over to see what was happening. The parents eagerly waited for the reaction of the team. After a few minutes, the news was obviously about ready to be shared with the team. Sure enough, the team erupted in cheers and they stood up and began jumping around like popcorn. To say were excited would be an understatement. Many of the parents were in tears at the faith placed in the team and the team reaction. The second the news was shared, I knew no matter what happened for the rest of the season, this opportunity would stay with Peppermint forever.

Being the young naïve children they were, they did not yet realize what a gift they had been blessed with. All they knew is that they were going up against the big kids and they needed to do their very best to not only win the Youth Large division but also score high enough in Level 1 to win an at-large bid to go to Summit. It was a very tall order but this team had overcome the impossible many times and they were up for the challenge one more time.

There were a few risks in making this decision. Competing as a youth team would mean that they would have to forfeit the possibility of winning the triple-crown point race. Although Mint was competing at UCA they would not be competing as a mini team, therefore ineligible to win in their respective division. They would also be going up against a very strong youth large team that had already won a summit bid at Cheersport. It would be a risky move, but with UCA being the final competition it was worth a shot.

Upon making this decision Peppermint would have to modify the team. In order to compete in the youth large division Peppermint would need at least 21 athletes to qualify as a large team. Word spread quickly about the news and we had a gym full of volunteers that wanted to help Peppermint. It was very exciting for everyone. One of the challenges of competing as a youth team was height. Peppermint overall was a pretty young mini team and we needed some height to offset some of our younger Peppermints. Coach Ashley consulted with some of the Stingray youth team coaches along with the parents of those athletes. With permission from all, the team of eighteen would soon be twenty three. Adding teammates can be a risky move as teams build bonds and learn how the maximize strengths and weaknesses over the course of the year. Selecting the right mix into this team would be critical as the new members would only have three short weeks to learn the routine and be flawless.

Coach Ashley introduced the new members of the team, and Peppermint was so excited to have them join. What was most exciting to them was all the new members of the team were Peppermint alumni. The new members of the team were extremely excited as they had an additional opportunity to go to summit with Peppermint along with their current team. While the team was excited, there was no time to waste. The team began walking through the routine with the new team members and the coaching staff had to begin to reconfigure the routine for the new additions. The trick for the coaches was to limit any major changes to the routine but also keep the wow factor and intensity for the Level 1 routine. It would certainly be a change for the new athletes joining the team. They would now have the pressure of mastering two routines with each of their teams for the upcoming UCA competition.

As the new team began working on perfecting their chemistry. As team dad, I wanted to make sure the new parents of the new athletes felt welcomed and appreciated. We knew the new team members had a tough challenge of perfecting a brand new routine in which they had only five practices left to learn. It was no secret that the team and the parents had formed a special bond over the course of the season and I wanted to make sure we extended a warm welcome to everyone including the parents. The amount of sacrifice any cheer parent makes is significant. To add on the additional responsibility of committing to another team it was certainly a lot, we were all very appreciative. The new Peppermints volunteered to come in early and stay late to learn the new routine. Add this on top of practicing with two teams, their normal additional tumble classes and juggling school. It was really incredible to watch.

As practices progressed the entire gym learned about what Peppermint was going to attempt at UCA. Some of the parents did not quite understand how the Summit bid process worked, which created some uneasiness with parents on other teams. Some of the parents on other teams did not quite understand why Peppermint was throwing away the opportunity to win the points race for the triple-crown. Some parents felt there was no way the Peppermint a "Mini" aged team would earn an "At-Large" Summit bid as a youth team. There were many whispers going around the gym, but overwhelmingly the reactions were extremely positive, especially on the Stingray practice mats.

Many of the senior teams caught wind of what Peppermint was going to attempt at UCA and they did nothing but support and encourage Peppermint in gym, and via Twitter and it really made them feel special. The talent on every team at Stingrays is incredible at every level, but the older kids knew this team was special. They know what it feels like to be on a younger team and not necessarily get all the attention. They remember falling in love with cheer at a young age. They remember the exuberance and innocence of going out there with their team and just doing your best with the person to the right and left of you and creating memories. They understand what it feels like to be small in size, but giving undeniable trust in their teammates. They remember the innocence of feeling as special as Orange, Peach or Steel after running off stage after they hit their routine, because that is who you looked up to. They understand the bond that is "The Stingray Allstars" legacy. They understand that Peppermint will do their job because that is all they know, and that is all they have been coached to know. It seemed at this point Peppermint had convinced each other to perform on stage like nobody was watching. They knew they had entire Stingrays family behind them, big kids, coaches and all. If they failed, there would be disappointment but they knew the Stingrays family always had their back.

In return, Peppermint would give the other teams all they could from an encouragement stand point. Anytime Peppermint got the opportunity to watch the senior teams go full out, the entire team would scream out their music and watch intently as the older teams worked their magic and flew through the air with elegance and grace. Peppermint had memorized almost all of the other teams' music out of respect and admiration for the other teams in their gym. They loved all the teams, but Peach was special. The bond was undeniable and they would support each other every chance they got. The coaches helped support the effort as well. Many would come over to offer support and make suggestions and offer encouragement.

The new Peppermints were picking up the routine quickly, the entire team was bonding and the confidence in each other was quickly making itself appear on the practice mat. Full out after full out, Peppermint was hitting again and again. Occasionally there were a few timing issues or a small bobble or glitch, but for the most part the team was very close to being ready. The hard work was paying off and now we would soon see how the team would respond to the new division, added pressure and expectations.

The fun part was listening to the kids talk about the opportunity. They would often say things like "I can't wait until we get our opportunity to try and go to "Worlds." To them, Summit was their Worlds. Of course, Worlds is reserved for Senior Teams, but Peppermint watched every move at worlds on ESPN and that was all they knew. The new older additions got caught up in the hype and how could they not. This team had an incredible confidence about them and the culture was infectious. It seemed the team had a "nothing to lose" aura about them which was a great attitude to take into the last major competition of the year. At the end of the day, at any level, cheer has to be fun and this team made watching them a blast. A few of the Peppermints caught wind that they may be over their head with competing against youth teams and that only fueled the fire to work harder. Adding the moniker of "Underdog" made them even more dangerous and they thrived on the challenge.

It was only fitting that the last night of practice the teams had a full out party in preparation for UCA. The intensity level at the gym was intense as there were a few more Stingray teams striving for a Summit bid at the final competition of the year. Peppermint waited their turn to take the floor and passionately cheered on the other teams going full out. Peach was next, and you could see the banter between the two teams. Peppermint as a whole was so proud to call them their buddies and could not wait for them to hit the floor so they could cheer them on. As usual, Peach lit up the mat and showed the entire gym how to hit their routine, and without a second of hesitation Peppermint screamed out the final "I GOT 99 PROBLEMS BUT A PEACH AINT ONE!" in unison to close out the final full out for Peach. The dance started and Peppermint clapped to the beat of the music.

Normally, not too many teams would like to follow Peach but Peppermint pranced out there and was ready to attempt to equal the intensity level. Sure enough, they began their final full out, and in true

Peppermint fashion they hit and hit strong. The teams roared for them and they smiled together once last time as a new unit. It was time to take what they had learned and see what they could do at UCA.

11 UCA

As families made their way to UCA and the competition schedule came out, many of the parents including myself completed the due diligence to find out who we were competing against. Upon researching, we found out one of the teams had already won a full paid bid to Summit by winning Cheersport and outperforming many of the Level 1 teams in Atlanta , Georgia for the Large Youth Division. The competition was going to be tough. At this point in the year everyone was vying for the final bid positions and Peppermint could end up winning the Youth Large division at UCA and still not end up receiving a bid to summit. Not only did they have to win, but they also needed to outshine all Level 1 teams from Youth, Junior and Senior divisions in order to be considered for a bid, a very tall order for this young team.

Of course, we did not share any of this with Peppermint. They already knew week after week they were going to be up against the best. They already knew they were going to be underdogs going in to win, much less win an at large bid to summit. They knew what was expected of them and they did not need any more pressure, just reassurance to do their best.

At this point in the season when the "little minis that could" get into the zone, it was lights out. We only prayed they would be able to duplicate their performance two more times and make believers out of the new additions that they could in fact make this happen one more time.

We began hearing that Peppermint was gaining quite a following as word spread about their quest. We started receiving words of encouragement around the nation from Twitter, Fierceboard and other methods including a very touching letter we received from a little girl in Massachusetts. The letter appeared at Stingrays and caught the eye of one of our parents who was touched that a little girl so was inspired to write a letter to her favorite gym. The letter began by stating that Stingrays was her favorite gym in the whole world. (Other than her own) she mentioned the fabulous teams that make Stingrays so special. Orange, Steel, Peach and then she mentioned how she loves absolutely everything about Peppermint. The note went on to say that it would make her day if someone from

Orange could write back in their spare time. The parents were so touched by her simple note and flattered that they mentioned Peppermint. We as a parent group made it our mission to include our special little fan in our journey. We collaborated as parents and rounded up special items from all her favorite teams Orange, Peach, Steel and Peppermint and sent a care package to let her know we received her note. One of the parents actually spoke with the girls' mother and became friends on Facebook so she could follow the progress of her favorite teams via social media. The entire letter was very touching and a few of the girls from each of the teams actually became friends via social media as well, including a few of the Peppermints. The parents assured the girl we would keep her up to date on all her favorite teams as it was almost time to head down for the final competition.

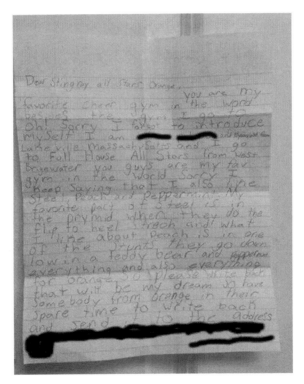

Written Letter from One of our Favorite Fans

It was the middle of March and the weather was gorgeous for the drive down to Orlando. Many of the families extended their trip and left a day early to enjoy the parks at Disney. This competition had a bit of a different vibe as the routine was pretty much set in stone. The typical pressure of hoping everyone made it on time and was accounted for on travel day was a bit different as almost the entire team was present a day early. What also helped is that the team has a pleasant distraction before the competition. Peppermint was able to bond at the swimming pool or head out together to the theme parks. The vibe seemed a bit looser and more relaxed than a normal competition. By early Friday afternoon the entire team was accounted for. I carefully crafted a text message to all the parents reminding them to get the team to bed at a respectable hour. I reiterated the entire plan for the next morning meet time, where to meet and what was going to happen best I could for the following day. I also reminded the parents we would be entering the ESPN Wide World of sports and it is a very busy venue so plan for traffic.

As we arrived early Saturday morning and ESPN Wide World of Sports was buzzing. Busses from teams all over the nation were arriving. The parking lot was filling up quickly as thousands of All Star cheerleaders and their parents descended on the venue. This was many of the Peppermints first time competing at UCA and the competition is very different in nature. The venue is beautiful and for the most part everything is outside except for the competition arenas. The team seemed very excited as they all began to trickle in at our morning meeting destination. My "Team Dad" back pack was out and ready for the normal typical small emergencies such as a lip stick touch up, ibuprofen for headaches (normally from parents) finger nail polish remover, nail clippers, and extra bow and socks just in case. As I complete roll call and count the final few Peppermints arriving everyone seems in great spirits. The team was allowed to take off their warm ups early as the weather was warming up in the Florida sun. The newly formed team gathered as they normally do, but this time there were a few new groups as the new members of Peppermint were included in the pre competition fun. It was validation of the warmth and acceptance exhibited by the entire team all year. Peppermint included everyone, and it only solidified the team bond even more. As the team lined up for warm ups the parents said their final good byes. The team lined up and away they went. Beecher gave a final hug to his mom, gave me a smile and a high five. The next time we would see them they would be trying to do the impossible for the first time competing in the Youth division.

As we waited for the team to perform, the parents all congregated in the ESPN restaurant located within the venue. There were a number of Stingray parents from other teams who noticed us all sitting together and went out of their way to come over and wish our team luck. We also spoke with parents from random gyms that were competing in various different divisions. They came over to wish us luck and heard about Peppermint going up in an age group and thought it was the coolest thing. Many of the parents asked how we as a parent group were holding up. They wanted to know if the team was nervous, if they were excited, some wanted to know how long it took them to perfect their stunt. It was flattering that people were so in tune with what our kids were doing. They wanted to know which venue they competed in so they could watch. It was great to bond with all of the parents both Stingrays and non-Stingrays it really speaks to the comradery of the sport.

One of the parents could not help the irony of being at Disneyworld and the team nickname being Minnie Mints and Mickey. It seemed fate could be on the side of this team but there was still a long way to go. As it inched closer to performance time, we all headed toward the venue to find seats. I caught up with the team as they were making their way into the venue from warm ups. I was asked to help keep the team assembled up in the stands. The entire crew was in such good spirits they did not seem nervous at all, but were pretty amped up. It is very interesting how young children vent their nervous energy. They could go from laughing hysterically to crying hysterically in the matter of seconds. Although they were a great team, they were still young kids. The quicker we could get them back stage the better. They did well with structure; unfortunately hanging out with me was not structure. At this point of the season, I was viewed more as the crazy uncle for the entire team. I pulled out all the stops trying to keep the team together. Sally Walker the Telephone game, nothing worked. I had to come up with something quick. We started the "dance party in your seat" game and thank God that struck a chord. Luckily that game bought me five minutes before the coaches finally took the team. I am sure it was quite entertaining for the parents surrounding the team watching me trying to keep the kids entertained. With all the chaos over, the team disappeared behind the curtain and we were moments away from day one.

The teams began performing and it was different not paying attention to all the mini teams. We watched them, but not with the same excruciating intensity. We did not watch them intently because most of us were wringing our hands with nervousness. When you are waiting for your team to perform everything else becomes a blur and background noise, it is really hard to explain as a parent. The mini teams finished and it was now time for the Youth division to perform. Peppermints competition took the floor and it was the team that had already won their paid bid to summit. The routine was very strong. Peppermint had their work cut out for them. The amoeba of Stingray contingency was streaming into the arena. Emotions became overwhelming for the Peppermint parents as they watched hordes of people fighting to get into the packed arena to watch Peppermint. No matter what happened, the amount of pride emitted by the parents of this mini team would be indescribable. They were about to take the stage as a youth team for the first time and you could see them peeking from behind the curtain and they were dying to get out on the mats.

As the team inched toward the on deck area you could see the excitement emitting from the team. They wanted to show everyone what they had. You got the feeling that they knew they really had nothing to lose at this point. Coach Ashley led the Stingray coaching contingency out from behind the curtain. We were all trying to read her face to get a read on how the warm up session went. She seemed very focused but loose. She did not seem worried at all, as she focused all of her attention to the stage. Once the coaches arrived, there was a mad dash to the front of the stage from the parents. The PA announcer introduced Peppermint and they stormed the stage beaming with smiles and waved to crowd that was roaring for them. They seemed a bit overwhelmed by all the energy of the crowd. As they all settled in to their spots for the opening, you could see most of the team stopping for only a second to take in the moment. This was a big crowd for them. Coach Ashley re adjusted a few of the Mints to make sure they were positioned perfectly. You could see there smiles widen as they knew it was about time. The eternal pause and gap of silence began to put me on the edge of my knees waiting for them to start. Then a slight head nod from Coach Ashley and then came the thumbs up. It was go time. The music blared and the now famous "WELCOME TO MINTLAND" blared as the opening section of the music started. Peppermint flew into action with an attitude I have never seen before. They were on fire and hit the opening with such confidence and sass. The entire team was clearly in the zone. They prepared for the stunt of death and the entire parent section gave a collective gasp as they went up and rocketed down in sequence one by one. The team was making the routine look effortless as they flew through the air and tumbled flawlessly. The facial expressions and attitude were contagious and the arena roared with approval. The team rocketed into the dance section of the routine and they knew it was a good one. You could see a couple of the mints begin to cry during the dance as the emotion rushed through their bodies as the routine was coming to an end. With the final jump though to forward roll Beecher polished off the routine landing in the middle of the stage surrounded by his crew with a beaming smile.

The music abruptly stopped and the crowd roared with approval. They knew it was a good one. The team tried to collect themselves to get off the stage, but most felt compelled to hug each other. They were pumped as they hit again. They quickly ran off the stage and were warmly welcomed by the entire coaching staff. Coach Ashley did a good job to try and temper their enthusiasm, as with any good team, over confidence can be just as destructive as no confidence. The team watched the replay of the routine and the coaches carefully critiqued a few things they could improve on for the following day. We passed out some treats for the team so they could celebrate their great performance.

Immediately the team began to ask how the other teams looked. As always, we shared the truth. "They looked really good, but so did you." One of the kids asked if they looked too little on stage. I laughed and said, "No, you guys looked larger than life." Then one of the Mints stated that Peach was about to perform in the "Milk House" and everything stopped. Word spread like wildfire and the entire team ran to their parents to ask if they could go watch their big sisters light up the floor. Without hesitation we all began to make our way over to the large pavilion where Peach was performing.

As we got closer to the arena we ran into numerous Stingray families who all stopped to ask us how we did and were wishing us luck as we shared the news that we "hit zero deductions." The sea of people leading into the arena was intimidating for the kids. The arena holds over 5000 people and it was standing room only. Much of the team had to separate to find seats and we all were trying to settle in as a few of the

Senior Medium 5 teams were performing. As expected, the competition was fierce as the senior teams complete breathtaking combinations of tumbling stunting and dance. The arena was rocking with excitement as each team competed to be the best on that day.

As many of the teams finished up you could tell Peach was coming up soon. The arena was noticeably more active and you could see people scurrying around the arena trying to get a better spot in anticipation of Peach taking the mats. At this stage of the season the secret was out. Peach was the team to beat as they won the first two stages of the Triple Crown in the Medium Senior 5 division. The arena was bursting to watch Peach perform. At that point it hit me, and I looked over at my oldest daughter and said. "Can you believe all these people waiting to watch Peach perform? You are so lucky to be able to practice with them every week and watch them up close and in person." She responded, "Yeah they are our friends and big sisters." She smiled and looked down upon the stage beaming with pride. I looked out and the Mints were spread out throughout the arena. The coaches made their way to the designated area in front of the stage. A few of the Mints tried to scream to get the coaches attention to wish them luck and let them know that they were cheering them on as they always did. Coach Aaron noticed a few of the Mints up in the stands and gave them a little wave and smile. The mints began to jump up and down excited that Coach Aaron noticed them.

The PA announcer began to speak and the kids were all on the edge of their seats. The PA system roared "AND NOW FROM MARIETTA, GEORGIA...... The Stingray Allstars PEACH" All of the Mints immediately stood up and began screaming there little lungs out, but this time it was different. The roar of the Milk House crowd drowned out the cheers from the little mini team that had consistently had their back all year. Peppermints spirit and love transcended the noise of the crowd, it was too strong to be drowned out and they emanated a spirit from their seats that very clearly was felt all the way down on the floor.

As the standing room only crowd watched the magical squad do their thing, I scanned the crowd and observed all the Mints in various parts of the arena singing every word of the now famous music. When it came time for Peppermints favorite part of the music, magically the entire arena erupted by screaming " I GOT 99 PROBLEMS BUT A PEACH AINT

ONE!" as if almost to salute the friendship of the two teams. The Peppermints all smiled and jumped to the beat of the music as they watched their favorite team complete another flawless performance.

As the crowd was going berserk, Peach filed off the stage with elegance and grace. It was time to re-group and get focused for the second day of the competition. As it always does, the adrenaline rush of competing and watching other teams begins to wear off and the crash effect of that waning adrenaline comes fast and with a vengeance. It was time to head back to the hotel for some relaxation. As we were walking back to the parking lot we were overwhelmed with the amount of people randomly congratulating us and giving us best wishes for day 2. Word spread that Peppermint hit and the question was, could they do it again on day 2, and would it be good enough to earn an at large bid?

We did our best to maintain the normal competition routine. We as a family let the kids play and relax a little bit by the pool. Then we started an early dinner with friends and other Stingray parents. The trick was to keep the team humble and focused and we as a parent group were pretty good at this stage of the season. I drafted out the final group text of the competition to all the families. I slowly began to get a few responses from some of my favorite parents.

The parents were very upbeat and the texts ran through a gamut of emotions of hope, anxiety, and fear. When you are alone in a hotel room with your child, as a parent, you are not able to share the emotion you are feeling with anyone else because you are protecting the fragility of your child's confidence. You are always second guessing your emotions as your child will feed off of your behavior, but inside, your emotions are running rampant. It is even tough to share what you are feeling with your own spouse in the same hotel room because you are constantly mindful of your child's presence. The only safe outlet for therapy and expression is often through text message to other parents and confidants.

I did my best to keep my responses positive yet humble. The only thing we could control at this point was do the best we could to get our children to bed, and hope they were in the best spirits to do their best in the morning. We knew there would be a different routine in the morning. On day two the Peppermints would perform at Hollywood Studios at the

Indiana Jones arena. Not a huge change but enough to make everyone a bit nervous.

The next morning was upon us. Everyone was up bright and early and the mass exodus began as everyone made their way to the venue. Tension was easily diverted as the families each made their way toward the entrance of the theme park. The Peppermints were all smiles as they gathered for potentially their last time as a group.

As I started the final roll call, I knew what this meant, but I did not want to accept reality. I scanned over all twenty three kids and began to get very sentimental. I was so very grateful for everything the team had done all year, including welcoming me with open arms as they have done with everyone who came in contact with them all year. I did not want the season to end, but I knew the odds. I wanted them to do the impossible and extend their season. Everyone felt the same way, I could tell from the demeanor of the parents. Destiny was in this teams favor, but you always have a hint of anxiety. This was the little mini team that could. We were one more two minute and thirty second routine away from performing and learning our destiny.

Unfortunately, we were still a few hours from the team taking the stage. The parents escorted the team toward the venue as a group. We kept the kids corralled the best we could for the coaches. The entire team was accounted for and they were in great spirits. We were admiring the innocence of the moment as the team only focused on playing with each other, smiling and laughing while having fun together as a group. Never once did we get the sense that anyone was nervous or worried about what they were about to attempt. The parents were clearly more nervous than the kids and something was about to give. The parents kept asking me when the coaches were going to take the kids. They had been bottling up their emotions all evening. It seemed the parents wanted to separate themselves so they could vent to each other and blow off some steam.

The coaches made their way over to the group and began to signal that it was about time to head out to warm ups. As the kids gathered, I don't think they realized this could be the last performance together. It was just not the way they were trained to think. They just knew they had to go out and do their best and that would make everyone happy. The parents started to group together. One of the parents asked me if I wanted to go with them after the kids were released. I asked, "Where are you guys headed?" She just responded, "Just follow us". As soon as the coaches gave us the all clear and led the team toward warm ups a large group of parents made a mad dash for the "Tower of Terror." Clearly the parents needed to blow off some steam and Hollywood Studios was an awesome place to do it.

After a bit of fun, it was getting closer to performance time. We began jockeying our way toward the front of the venue and lower and lower in the stands as the other teams performed. The venue was outside and the sun was beaming in from the back of the arena. We watched as all the teams performed and they were good. Our family made its way to the front row of the arena backed by the entourage of Peppermint parents. As Peppermint made their way into the staging area we could see their heads popping up in the background. They seemed extremely excited to make their way to the exciting new venue. After watching Peach perform the day before, they must have felt like they were on cloud nine. Not only did Peppermint share the same uniforms as Peach but they also wore the same glitter paint along the side of their face. As the Mints heads kept peeking over the wall, the flashes of the glitter paint were fluttering as the sun hit their face.

As the PA announcer began to announce Peppermint, I took a big deep breath in a failed attempt to calm my nerves. The team stormed the stage with smiles and waves. You could not help but fall in love with the joy and innocence the team emanated. Coach Ashley, Coach Kelsey and Coach Jessica took their places in front of the stage. All eyes focused on Coach Ashley for the thumbs up. The music started and the team erupted into action. As they started my eyes intently focused on every motion the team made. My eyes darted from left to right, right to left scanning the entire stage. As a Dad it is tough to not just focus on your child, but as I have learned, Cheer is a team sport. In order to honestly assess the team performance you need to train yourself to watch the entire routine as a judge would. It was very tough to do between desperate gasps in between each successful stunt or tumbling pass. The tension was getting to me and we were only halfway home.

As the team entered into the pyramid phase of the routine they seemed confident and in control. My heart began to race more than usual. My eyes were fluttering back and forth scanning every move of the routine. My breathlessness turned into gasps for air as the seconds seemed to tick away as minutes. I knew the routine like the back of my hand, and I desperately kept looking for perfection with every scan of my eyes. If an arm fluttered or a foot seemed out of place, I tried to critique it within my head with the only split second I had until the next transition. As we inched towards the dance, I prayed nothing out of the ordinary happened. Peppermint seemed to look straight at the coaches and parents with a huge collective smile as to say "We got this." With confidence beaming, they nailed every count with a look of conviction. With the last few seconds of the routine I felt a release of pressure and the team that had not let us down all year, finished with authority. One of the new Peppermints who were overcome with emotions stood with her hands in the air making the praise emoji signal.

I looked at my wife and said, "I think they did it, did you see anything out of place?" She responded, "No, they looked incredible again." With that, I immediately went back behind stage to help gather the team and get them organized. I wanted to bring the team up to the coaches so they could watch the replay of the routine. Peppermint began to make their way off the stage and I noticed one of the Mints in hysterics. The team surrounded her as they tried to figure out what the issue was. Coach Ashley came over to ask her what happened as we feared she may have been hurt getting off the stage.

She stated she dropped one of her body positions to quickly and she thought they were now going to lose because of it. Everyone assured her that it was fine and nothing looked out of place. She calmed down a bit and they began to watch replay of the routine. As the routine was displayed the Coaches gave recognition and positive feedback as the team displayed excellent execution. When it came to the section of the routine that was in question, we all focused on the athlete. What I saw, I could not believe. Coach Ashley said, "See, there was no deduction there. You did great!"

What the little mint was referring to was something that many of the parents could not see. I saw it on the replay and only noticed it because I was so familiar with the routine. In one of the stunts, the flyers go up into a scale and her leg was maybe an inch and a half lower than the other three flyers. While it was not 100 percent perfection it was far from a deduction. My first thought was how incredibly impressed I was that this team was so in tune with their routine, that they knew within an inch or two if it was not perfect. It was a testament to the coaching and dedication from this team.

Coach Ashley finished the team meeting by stating how incredibly proud she was of the team effort. She reaffirmed that the team did their best and that is all she could ask. She let us know to re convene at 10:00 am for awards. One of the Mints raised their hand to ask a question. Coach Ashley called on the mint. She stated, "Ok so you did say we did our best right? Does that mean we can have Dippin Dots?" The team erupted in cheers and Coach Ashley gave them a huge smile and said "Well I will leave that up to your parents." Needless to say many of us had a Dippin Dots brunch on that morning.

About an hour later the team began to reemerge from different corners of the theme park for the upcoming awards ceremony. Everyone was in good spirits and the team was clearly having fun at Hollywood Studios. The team gathered together and we made our way toward the lower left corner of the venue as a team. We waited for the final teams to compete and then once instructed made our way down to the arena floor. The team was buzzing with anticipation and nervous energy. All of the Level 1 teams that competed in the Youth Division in the morning gathered on the stage. The announcer began to rattle off the winners in the other divisions. Peppermint waited patiently and showed great sportsmanship as all the teams do cheering for everyone who competed.

It was time for the Youth Large division awards and everything seemed to be a blur. Everything seemed to move so fast and the next thing you know the MC was about to announce the second place finisher for the division. I scrambled to remove my phone from my pocket to capture the moment. What ever happened we knew we could be proud of what this team accomplished whether they won or not. As I began filming with my phone, the announcer began to say the name of the team. All I could do was look down at Peppermint. I wanted to remember the moment good or bad. Whether they won or lost it would not matter. In my mind they proved they could compete at the higher level.

The announcer began to speak and I felt my body wince with

anticipation as I held my breath, awaiting the fate of our team. Playing back the routine in my head one more time to think if there was anything I missed. Then it happened. The MC announced the name of the team for second place. It was not Peppermint. I froze and then I watch Peppermint freeze. They all wanted to spontaneously combust but they could not. They have been trained and coached so well. Out of respect for the second place team, Peppermint sat in complete silence and as still as they possibly could. They all locked arms to help each other contain their excitement as they cheered on the second place team. As the team cleared the stage you could tell the anticipation of the pending announcement was too much to handle. The Mints began to pop up and down on their knees like jumping beans in anticipation of the final announcement. The announcer bellowed and your winner in the Youth Large Level 1 division. Peppermint from the Stingray Allstars! The team erupted in cheers and they shot up out of their kneeling position in unison. The team collected themselves and made their way over to pick up the banner and trophy as a team.

The excitement was too much for some and tears of joy streamed down many of the Peppermints faces. The team headed back stage toward the champions section to receive their Champions jackets. I was tasked with organizing the team in reverse height order shortest to tallest. As I organized the team I started to walk toward the back of the line. Most of the new Peppermints were towards at the back and I noticed one of the new Peppermints seemed much more emotional than the rest of the team. I asked her if she was ok. I was not sure if she was hurt or did not feel good. She responded, "I am just so happy, I did not realize I get to keep the Champions jacket." The team gave her a huge hug to comfort her. I was so proud of the team for embracing the new Mints. I know it meant a lot to be accepted by the entire group. Honestly, we were so lucky to have them help. They truly complemented the team and made them stronger as a whole. It was a moment I will never forget.

After everyone received their awards we took a few pictures and then the focus turned to the elephant in the room. One of the kids asked and all the parents were wondering the same thing. When do they make the bid winners announcements? Coach Ashley informed the group that she believed the announcement would be made at 4:30pm in the same venue. She released the team to their parents and I informed them that I would try and confirm and send out a text message to verify. The team dispersed and the families made their way back out to the theme park to take in a few hours of fun before we needed to be back for the announcements at 4:30.

Our family ate lunch and began to take in some fun at Hollywood Studios. My youngest wanted to ride some of her favorite attractions and my oldest wanted to ride one of the roller coasters. Since my little one was too small for the roller coaster we decided to split up as a family. My oldest daughter wanted to go with one of her older Stingray friends to wait in line for the Rockin Roller coaster. We told them they needed to be back in a few hours so we did not miss the bid announcements. She agreed and went off with her friend and their family.

My wife and youngest daughter headed toward the Toy Story ride which was a favorite of my youngest. We got in line at about 1:20pm. While waiting in line, I received a frantic text from one of the parents who were watching other teams in the arena. "They are making the Youth Level Bid announcements in 5 minutes!" I froze and texted her back immediately. "Are you sure they said 4:30?" She responded, "I am positive I just heard the announcement. I am sitting in the arena now." As fast as I could I quickly pecked out a group text to everyone to make their way back to the arena ASAP. My wife and I grabbed my youngest and darted back to the Indiana Jones Theatre. It was going to be close but we should be able to make it in time for the announcement. On the way back I started receiving frantic texts from parents who were still eating lunch or stuck in line for a ride or on a ride currently. My heart broke for them as I knew they would not be able to make it from across the park in time. My only hopes were that they stalled out the ceremony and announcements so everyone could make their way to the arena in time. My thoughts immediately shifted to my own Peppermint. My oldest daughter was with one of her friends who did not have a cell phone. There was no way to alert her in time for her to watch the ceremony and announcements. We scrambled to the venue and arrived about halfway through the normal award ceremony for the competing teams. The bid announcements would take place at the end of the award ceremony.

One by one frantic parents and Peppermints began arriving to watch the ceremony completely drained and exhausted from running across the theme park. The award ceremony concluded and the announcer said they would announce the At Large and Paid Summit bid winners momentarily. I was scanning the arena to see if any more Peppermints or parents showed up. I was torn about the situation. I could not help but think it may be better if the team were not present if they didn't win an at large bid, but I cringed at the thought of them not being able to experience the moment if they were awarded such an honor.

The music cascaded in theatrics and a loud drum roll emitted from the sound system. The announcer began to speak and my wife switched her phone on to video the moment for the parents who were not going to be able to see the result. The MC shouted "And the winner of the at large bid to summit is PRO ATHLETICS!" The crowd erupted for the youth team who won from a small gym. My heart sank, I was crushed. I dropped my head down between my knees and my youngest daughter learned over and said, "They did not get it did they Daddy?" I said "No honey they did not" The announcer continued and moved on to the second announcement. He shouted, "And your PAID SUMMIT BID WINNER THE STINGRAY ALLSTARS......" The announcer said the team name but with the eruption of screaming I could not hear the actual Stingray team that won. We had three potential teams that could have been awarded the honor. We stopped filming immediately to try and find out the answer. I ran to the top of the steps looking for anyone who heard what the announcer said. I tried to replay the recording to make out what he said. My youngest daughter tugged on my shirt and said, "Daddy, THEY SAID PEPPERMINT!" I collapsed from disbelief. There was mass confusion on the announcement as no one made out what the announcer said. I stopped and immediately texted Coach Ashley, "DID WE JUST GET A PAID BID?" She responded, "It sure sounded like it."

I began walking around in complete shock. They did it. Not only did Peppermint get a bid to Summit but the team was awarded a full paid bid in the Youth Division. Meaning Peppermint outscored every Level 1 team that competed in all age groups. It was a miracle and an amazing feat. Never did we dream the team would earn a paid bid. We were just hopeful to earn and at large bid.

We were looking to share the news as fast as we could. I turned to twitter to make the announcement as I knew the families who were making their way to the arena would be glued to twitter looking for any sign of an announcement. The second I tweeted the results, I began receiving rampant alerts of retweets and favorites from around the nation. So many people were eagerly anticipating the bid results for this "little mini team that could".

We ran into the first few parents and a few were trembling with emotion. Peppermints were running everywhere hugging each other and crying tears of joy. It was truly a once in a lifetime experience. Unfortunately, my daughter and a few other Peppermints did not make it back in time to experience the good news. One by one the families made their way back to the arena and we were able to share the news with the ones who did not already know. About 30 minutes later my oldest daughter made her way back to the arena. I slowly walked up to her and calmly shared that they had won a paid bid to Summit. She looked up at me, smiled, and said "Yeah I know, about 10 people told me on the walk back here." I looked her right in the eye and shared that I was so very proud of her and her team."

After a fun day at the park we all started back to the hotel. Many of the older teams heard the news and were all making the Peppermints feel like celebrities. Many of the Mints wore their Championship jackets even though it was still very warm out. Everyone was extremely excited for them. It was truly an incredible weekend for all.

12 THE ROAD TO SUMMIT

The day following UCA many of the Mints made their way to Stingrays for tumble classes and the excitement had not yet worn off. The kids came running into the gym with their distinctive UCA championship jackets. As the parents began to head up to the observation room, curiosity began to take over. Many of the parents began looking at who would be competing at Summit which was only a month and a half away. Summit is an invitation only competition that seats the best teams at each level from across the nation. Some of the parents were still trying to understand what just happened from the previous 72 hours. It all still seemed like a blur.

Parents had to adjust a few things as our season had just been extended by almost two more months with the preparation to go to Summit. This part of the journey was not in the cards as of two weeks ago. It was a high class problem to have. We were very grateful to have the opportunity to represent Stingrays at Summit. More importantly, we were forever grateful as parents that the coaching staff had the faith in our children to give them this gift that would last a lifetime. The team really did not fully comprehend what they accomplished. To them it was just another competition. It would take some time of reflection and age to be able to look back and say, we were the team that did this. The team wanted to represent themselves as best they could at Summit it was going to take a lot of work to do well. The team and the parents were up for the challenge.

Coach Ashley sent out a very detailed plan for me to share with the parents that covered the next two months. At Peppermints first practice Coach Ashley sat the team down and shared her plan for Summit. After a few minutes of observation, it was evident that the routine was going to be completely re-worked. It was clear that the team was excited to try something new. At this point, Peppermint had nothing to lose and it was time to go for broke. The team had ridden their signature routine all year and it was time to shake things up. They had taken risks all year, why stop now?

There were whispers of concern from around the gym about changing the routine. Some people were concerned that with such a young team the coaches should stick with the routine that brought them to the dance. It was a fair argument, but I knew exactly what the Coaches were going for. They knew this team had it in them and they were going to push this team to its limits and give them the best opportunity to go far at Summit. Coach Ashley told them all year that they were the best Mini team in the world and these kids believed her. They wanted to show everyone that with faith in your team, you can accomplish anything. The hard work began and you could tell this was not going to be easy. Many of the practices were very painful to watch. After you become used to watching a team hit practice after practice it was tough watching the opposite. Worried parents consoled each other and shared that we have been here before with "Stunt of Death." We kept telling each other to have faith in the team, they will get it, and they always have. It was different this time though. We did not have much time and only a limited number of practices to make sure we perfected the new stunts and routine.

Over the course of the next few weeks many of the team members would come early and stay late to work on the routine while juggling school and other activities. They worked as hard as they could and time was running out. The Summit showcase was coming up and the team was working hard to perfect the new ambitious routine. When it was on, it looked incredible when it went bad, it went really bad.

One of the parents who were not from Peppermint approached me with concern that they were not going to get it in time. After a few weeks of hearing this, I began to get a little frustrated. I stayed positive, but defended this team. I was watching the same thing they were, but I knew they would get it. My typical response back to people with concerns was, "With all due respect, I am not sure you know what this team is capable of. I know they have another gear and when they switch that gear on, they are unstoppable. You just watch." I could see the team was very close to getting on track they just needed to hit that Peppermint switch and they could make it happen. Coach Ashley knew exactly what the team needed. During one of the water breaks I watched Ashley walk over to the front floor of the Stingray gym. That could only mean one thing. She was heading over to talk with the coaches from Peach. After about 10 more minutes of preparation. The team made its way over to where Peach was practicing. It was time for a full out party.

The mints watched Peach go through their pre full out routine. Mint lined the edge of the mats as they have done all year to watch their favorite team. Peach hit the button and at this stage of the year Peach was absolutely on auto pilot. They made their routine look absolutely effortless. You could see the Peppermint getting more and more amped as they watch their mentors put on a clinic. As Peach completed yet another flawless routine, Peppermint took the floor with a bit more pep in their step. Peach took a moment to regroup and took a few words of what to do better next time from the coaching staff. After that, the entire focus was on the "little team that could." Peach let them have it with a resounding roar of encouragement. The attitude seemed to seep back into the core of the team and the music started and away they went.

As the parents stood up from their chairs to get a better look in the viewing area the routine seemed to be in slow motion as we analyzed each count of the routine. They began to pick up momentum with each completed stunt and tumble pass. The pyramid was flawless and the jumps were clean. With each second you could see Peppermint picking up confidence in each other and becoming one with the routine. The dance showed an extra once of pep, confidence and attitude as they hit the routine clean for the first time in full outs. The parents erupted in the viewing area and began clapping. Each team went through another full out and both teams hit again.

With about two weeks left before they left for Summit, they finally hit stride and now needed to maximize every opportunity to build confidence in practice. I thought to myself and smirked. I knew they had it. I was eager to have them show everyone else what they were capable of. As practice ended that night, I sauntered down to the entrance to wait on the team to be released as usual. On this particular night the team burst out of the gym with a distinct energy about them that signaled that they knew they were back. I waited for a bit as the excited team mingled a bit in the hallway. A few minutes later Coach Ashley walked into the main office and took a seat. I mentioned that they looked great tonight. She responded with a look of relief and said, "I think it's finally coming together, I am really excited for them."

The following weekend would prove to be an exciting one for The Stingray Allstars. After the final full out party between Peach and

Peppermint the Senior 5 team that adopted our mini level 1 team took their talents to The Cheerleading Worlds at the ESPN World Wide of Sports in Orlando, FL. Beaming with pride and anticipation the Peppermints were glued to their computer screens and TVs ready to watch their big sisters represent Stingrays in the Medium Senior Level 5 Division. It was destiny in the making as Peppermint watched every second of the routine and after about 1 minute into the routine you knew they were going to do it. As the team had done all year, Peach dominated the stage with a breathtaking performance as they went on to become World Champions.

The final week of practice was upon us and it was crunch time. The weekend prior the parents planned a very nice Summit sendoff party. The team was able to bond even more, and it was really a great time. All the speculation was over and the clock was running out. All the parents were completing due diligence trying to find videos of the competition to compare routines. While admirable, at this stage of the year it really did not matter. This was the best of the best. It would come down to execution, passion, and cleanliness. The final week the gym puts on a Summit Sendoff full out party to exhibit all of the teams making their way to "The Summit" it is a showcase for friends and family and included a ton of teams from Stingrays who were heading to summit. Peppermint was very excited to be included in this annual event. There was one more practice before the Summit send-off party.

Before the practice started I was sitting in the front lobby of Stingrays. A few of the Peppermints were chatting amongst themselves they seemed in deep discussion. One of the Peppermints saw me sitting on the couch with my daughter. She came over to me and looked very concerned. She began to ask me a question, "Mr. Eric, do you think we are going to do well at Summit?" I responded, "Of course you guys are going to do great at Summit, why are you asking me that?" She responded with a very concerned look. "Well someone said that it was a waste of time for us to go because we were too little and we would not be able to compete against the big teams."

My heart sunk... I know the realities of youth sports. I know unintentional things are said in passing that can be taken the wrong way both by adults and children alike. I felt a rush of frustration course through my body and then I became very emotional hoping their spirits were not crushed. I wanted to hunt down whoever said this to her, but I realized where she heard this was not important. The important thing at this second was that five Peppermints were surrounding her waiting for a response.

As I took a second to gather myself, I scooted up on the edge of the couch and began to respond, "Well the truth is, you guys have been proving people wrong all season long. At the beginning of the season people did not think you would be able to do your "stunt of death" they thought it was too hard for you to do, and you mastered it. Never in a million years would we think that you would win Grand Champion in most all of your competitions, but you did it. People also did not think you would be able to get an at-large Summit Bid, but you proved them wrong by doing even better and won a full paid bid. If you guys just believe in each other like you have all year, you guys are going to do great at Summit you just watch."

I prayed that response would cheer them up a bit. I waited for a response but there was nothing but deep thought. After a slight pause, the Peppermint looked up and gave me a quick hug and with that she turned and yelled c'mon guys. The Mints ran into the gym as a group. Those simple words of encouragement seemed to move them past the moment. As I took a deep breath relieved that the moment was over with, I walked upstairs and began to watch practice. The team was focused and began full outs with a chip on their shoulder. They ended that practice session with three hits in a row. It seemed the "little team that could" was back at it again. As they wrapped up that night it hit me. This was the final practice as a team. I began to reflect on the past 10 months and it was an intense feeling of emotion thinking about their growth. There was one more gathering as a team at the Summit Showcase and then it was off to Orlando.

The week flew by and it was time for the Summit Showcase. Stingrays would be taking a total of 23 teams to Summit. It was an impressive showing. The gym was packed with all of the teams, parents, and friends. The line to enter the building was wrapped around the back of the building. The team prepared as hundreds of people packed into the Stingrays main gym. It was a bit intimidating as all the teams clamored for floor space to warm up. Peppermint began to mark their routine and walk through as many times as they could. As the team was warming up many of the older kids from the other teams took time to share Peppermints story with significant others. They made a point to make sure the story was told, because at Stingrays we are all one big family and all of the teams have each other's back. The kids wanted to make sure people understood that even though they were by far the youngest team, they were going to compete and represent their gym. It was flattering that the kids did that. It gave the Mints a lift just when they needed it.

All of the teams performed and they looked spectacular. Peppermint wowed the crowd with their incredible energy and execution. It was now time for a special time of the night as all of the Peppermint parents had a special sendoff gift for the entire team after the exhibition. Coaches scoped out a corner of the gym to huddle in. We gathered the team and had them hold hands and make a circle. Once they were settled, we had them sit down and close their eyes. Once their eyes were closed, I began to hand out the Summit gift packets for each of the team members. The team was busting with anticipation to open their gifts. Once everyone had their gift in their lap, Coach Kelsey instructed the team to open their eyes. The teams opened their gifts and were very excited.

Peppermint Waiting for Summit Gifts

While that was happening, a group of people came over to see what was happening with Peppermint. It was the 2015 World Champions Peach. They took time out their busy school schedules and came to the Summit Showcase. They wanted to surprise Peppermint. The team stopped what they were doing with their gifts and began to wave to the team that became their friends all season. The team began to give each other hugs and many of the Mints had not seen the team since they became World Champions. It was such a small gesture but it was a moment that will last a lifetime in their minds. The little mini team felt ten feet tall as they were able to hang with their big sisters. Peach even let all of the mints wear their

World Championship medals. A few of the members from Orange who had befriended a few of the Mints came over to offer support as well. It was a very special moment they will never forget.

Summit Showcase Peppermint and 2015 World Champion Peach Rays

After the exciting Summit Showcase it was time to head to Orlando for Summit. The nice thing about Summit is that it would be at a familiar venue. Peppermint won their bid at the ESPN Wide World of Sports two months prior. Stingrays does a great job trying to keep the experience as uniform as possible. We stayed in the same hotel and followed pretty much the exact same routine as UCA.

The fever of Stingray families began the pilgrimage down to Orlando. Summit is set up a little different than a normal two day competition. Normally all teams that compete on day one will continue on to day two. At Summit teams have to qualify with a score high enough to move on to day two, typically this means a score in the top fifty percent of all teams competing on day one. That means a fatal mistake on day one could mean you go home and do not compete in day two. The goal for Peppermint was to try and make into day two finals. Competing in the youth division at Summit was going to be a huge challenge. We wanted to set reasonable expectations for this team heading into the competition. If they were able to make it to the finals at Summit that would be a huge accomplishment in itself.

It was the morning of day one and the drive to the venue was filled with silence. As the massive sea of humanity began to stream into the venue, I began looking for the distinctive neon yellow Summit shirts that were one of the gifts presented to all of the Stingray teams. Peppermints were scattered all over the front section of the park. Many were taking a moment to take a picture in front of the huge ESPN Wide World of Sport Globe that welcomes athletes from all over the world. One by one the Peppermints began to arrive at the designated meeting spot just inside the main gate. It is a typical Peppermint mantra to keep a low profile before a competition and keep distractions to a minimum. Fortunately, at the main entrance we saw many of other Stingray families entering the venue. The Mints had a very distinctive Red and White bow. It was a dead giveaway and everyone was coming over to wish Peppermint good luck. It was a great feeling to have the support from everyone. We also met people from other gyms who heard about the Mints story and came over to wish them well. It was great to meet other people from other parts of the country and learn about their team and story. It is really one of the special traits of competitive cheer.

It was now about time for the team to organize and head out to the football fields for warm ups. The smiles and laughter quickly turned into frantic last minute lipstick and hair touch ups. Last minute scrambling led to words of encouragement, hugs and kisses from Mom's, Dad's and other siblings. As each of the Mints began to gather themselves, I looked around to see many of the top Cheerleading coaches in the world surrounding this team of Level 1 cheerleaders offering support and encouragement. When you are surrounded by the caliber of coaches that Stingrays is blessed to have, sometimes you tend to take the pool of talent that surrounds you for granted. The parents noticed and thanked many of the coaches for coming by and offering support. The team began to line up in the usual formation. The smiles were replaced with stares of intense focus. Coach Ashley made the announcement that it was time to head out. I asked the coaches if they needed anything from the emergency bag before they left. They were good.

The team began to walk toward the practice area and the sea of Peppermint faithful erupted in cheers as the team began to walk away. Before they left, I went back to my buddy Beecher. I wished him good luck and told him to take care of our girls. He smiled and said, "I will" I gave him a high five and they were off.

The sea of humanity consumed the team as they disappeared into the long corridors of the venue. The waiting game was now upon us as the tight group of parents all lingered in the background. We slowly scattered in our own directions. Some of us are creatures of habit so we headed toward the restaurant we sat in at UCA. There was only an hour before we would need to head toward the venue. The parents seemed to be at ease with the situation for the moment. The team truly had nothing to lose at this point and since it was the last competition I think the parents wanted to try and enjoy the ride this time. We bonded by sharing stories that happened throughout the year. We had many good laughs and fond memories. As time wore on, it was time to head to the venue to find seats.

We all entered the arena and the tents were already packed and the competition had already begun in the other divisions. Watching the teams compete was awesome. You could feel the electricity and the intensity levels lifted from the teams currently performing. Teams were clearly pushing the limits and elevating their game to make it in to day two. We found seats off to the right hand side of the arena toward the back. The parents all filled in with hopes to move toward the middle on the stage once the other teams competed. It was about 15 minutes before Peppermint was scheduled to perform when I saw a few Peppermint bows pop up from behind the curtain. The coaches all walked out to the main viewing area where we were sitting. They all stood in the back and watched the teams perform. After one of the teams completed I looked over at Coach Ashley and I did not even have to say anything. She just looked and me and said, "They are ready to go" I looked down at the floor for what seemed like an eternity. The time was here, and that statement made it real.

The Mints one by one started appearing from behind the curtain and easing toward the staging area. They finally located the Peppermint entourage of parents and they erupted in smiles and waves once they saw everyone. With each step closer you could see the excitement building. They were focused and intensely dialed into the stage. They were so glad to be part of this. They wanted to show everyone they belonged here. They were certainly a dark horse in the field. Peppermint was announced to be up next. They huddled as group on their own, one last time before they hit the stage. They emerged from the huddle with an intense focus and sinister smiles; they were dialed in and fired up. They were assessing their competition and knew they had a shot.

The team before Peppermint finished their routine. It would be moments before Peppermint would take the stage. Parents scrambled for their positions in front of the stage. The coaches emerged and assumed their positions. The MC announced Peppermint and they aggressively took the stage with a look of determination and angst. They waved to the crowd and were bursting with smiles. After a few last minute position adjustments Coach Ashley gave the thumbs up and the music exploded through the sound system. They jolted into action as if they were shot out of a cannon. They had nothing to prove to anyone, but they were going to do it anyway. Thirty seconds into the routine was flawless. The "stunt of death" drew a new set of gasps from the new crowd that had never seen it before. After a minute in, the execution became even better with each eight count. Every ten seconds seemed like an eternity while watching with such intensity. The team went into autopilot for the rest of the routine and performed with an intense confidence that sold every motion and transition. The jumps for a Level 1 team did not seem human, and the pyramid oozed with perfect timing and execution as they made their way to the final dance. The Minnie Mints and Mickey danced like there was no tomorrow and they brought down the house. They wrapped up the performance of the year with a completely new routine that they just perfected in front of the Summit judges.

The music stopped and so did my heart. I collapsed to my knees and needed a minute to gather myself as the team did it once again. The Peppermint parents all did a collective embrace as the team began to make their way off the stage. Walking toward the designated meeting point to pick up the team you begin to hear things from people watching. The noise is non directional but you catch all the comments from people in the stands as you walk toward your destination. It is hard not to respond, but you hear them. "Oh, that was the mini team? They were awesome." "No way was that a mini team." "They are not even a youth team they should not even be here." You hear it all, but you can't engage in either the positive or negative comments. It is always best to let the performance do the talking, especially after an intense moment of watching your team. Coach Ashley followed me over to the side of the arena and she just shook her head. I could tell she was elated again.

The team disappeared behind the stage and the parents went out the back of the arena and around the side to wait for the team to be released. While waiting, all the parents were buzzing. We all had the same question on our minds, "Was that enough to make it to day two?" We all began asking if anyone saw anything out of place in the routine and the parents concurred they, hit zero deductions. Unfortunately, the parents do not judge cheer competitions. We watched the other teams competing and they were spectacular. Peppermint did all they could, it was all in the hands of the judges at this point.

The team emerged from the side of the building. All of them quickly scanning to find their parents, it was a an incredible feeling to watch the few seconds of desperation while each child tries to find their family and then the look of immediate joy overcomes them as soon as they finally lock eyes on their target. We as a family were waiting to see my daughter emerge. She stuck her head out of the building and frantically scanned the area looking for us. As soon as she found us she immediately darted our way, and gave us the biggest tackle hug she could. We all fell to the ground as a family in excitement. It was an incredible moment for all. The good news is that we would not have to wait too long to find out if Peppermint would make it to day two. The Summit Reveal would happen in about 45 minutes.

Coach Ashley released the team but requested to reconvene in about 30 minutes. The group immediately darted for the other Stingray teams who were warming up in the fields to offer support and blow off some steam the only way they knew how. They watched for a few minutes and then began stunting with each other and tumbling in the grass. After time had passed it was time to file back into the venue for the Summit reveal.

Everything was moving so fast. The team gathered alongside of the building and all of the coaches rounded up everyone. I completed a final head count to make sure we had everyone. Once again Peppermint disappeared as they were about to learn their fate. The teams all huddled on the stage. One by one each team made their way up to the performance floor. As the announcer began to speak I could feel the blood in my cheeks increase from warm to a boil. We prayed that the judges saw what we did on that stage, but knowing the other teams were just as deserving. The announcer wasted no time as he began announcing the Day two qualifiers from another division. The Large Youth Level 1 division was up next. As we waited patiently, all the parents began making eye contact with each other. We did not have to say anything at this point in the season, as we had formed a bond that would last forever during this journey.

The PA system erupted announcing the Youth Large division. He announced the first three teams and Peppermint was yet to be announced. He announced the forth team and my body went numb. My head collapsed between my knees as the announcer started speaking for the fifth and final time. If this was it, I was ok with it. They did the best they could, and went farther than anyone thought they could. Then it happened, he announced the fifth and team, and sure enough it was Minnie Mints and Mickey. My head shot up from between my knees and I almost passed out from the rush of blood. The parents section erupted in cheers as we were in disbelief and trembling with joy. We watched as the team bopped up and down together on stage. They made it to the finals it was official!

After the initial excitement wore off, we headed off to gather our team. The team was huddled up with Coach Ashley, Kelsey and Rupert. They emerged from the huddle excited but focused. I think the reality of the moment hit them and they realized they had a job to do. They were guaranteed a top five spot in the world. They wanted to make the most of it. Some parents had planned on breaking up the day by heading to the theme parks. Clearly, those plans needed to be altered. If I knew this coaching staff they were going to analyze the notes from the judges and craft a plan to work on what they needed to to fix.

Sure enough as the team broke their huddle. Coach Ashley summoned me over and said, "I will let you know specifics soon, but we will be planning on gathering the team for a mandatory practice soon. I will let you know as soon as I can." I nodded and assured her I would get the message out. We headed out to grab a bite of lunch. As we were eating, I received the text from Ashley. "Mandatory practice at the football fields at 5:30pm sharp" I sent out the group text and we were all set. We had a few hours before we had to be back. We headed back to the hotel for some rest and relaxation.

We arrived back at ESPN and headed for the our meeting destination. The park was still jam packed with thousands of cheerleaders competing on the day. We were stopped numerous times by Stingray families that heard the news via Twitter and other sources. All were so excited and congratulatory. You could see the Mints arriving from all corners of the park. Still not tall enough to emerge from the crowd you could see the distinctive red and white bows sticking up and parting the sea of humanity as they walked toward their destinations. As they arrived they immediately embraced one another and were excited to get going again. I was impressed with the maturity of the group as we could look at all of the major theme parks in the area. Never once did they complain that they had an extra practice. They were on a mission, and the hard work always paid off in the past.

Coach Ashley gathered the team together and she told the parents she would need the team for about and hour and a half. They took off hand in hand toward the football fields and took shelter on the far end of the fields under some shade. The parents all agreed it was time for a relaxing beverage. We all grabbed our favorite refreshing drink and made our way across the fields to sit in the bleachers together. We could see the team off in the distance practicing away.

As we watched, we bagan to re-live the entire season together. We had so many laughs talking about the great times we had over the course of the season. We spoke about how the kids have grown so much over the past ten months. We talked about how this experience was one they would never forget. We also talked about how the team could never really comprehend what they accomplished as human beings. The performances, medals, grand champion awards and jackets were nice. What was important to reflect upon is the genuine pleasant human beings this team had become. Encouraging all teams, befriending anyone around them and including everyone to make sure they were not left out. It was refreshing to see. We continued to discuss the impressive life lessons this entire season consisted of. We did not want the moment to end, so we continued to share great stories the entire time. After a while we began to look down upon our team. They were working hard as usual, but it seemed they were wrapping up. We watched as the team huddled one more time for the day. They began to break from the huddle. They slowly made their way back toward their parents some with arms around each other, some holding hands. I told the parents I would send out another reminder text this evening with specifics for the next day. We all went our separate ways and called it a night.

Day two began same as the day before except this day was a bit more emotional. As I opened my roll call app to make sure everyone was accounted for. I fought back the tears as I realized this would be the final time I would count heads for this incredible team. I could not believe how this team touched my soul. I was so grateful this team welcomed me the way they did. It was not normal for a Dad to be in this role, but I could not have been a part of anything better for me at this stage of my life. Today would conclude a chapter in history for this team, but we knew the soul of this team would continue on for years to come. I knew all the parents and coaches felt the same way.

Coach Ashley, Kelsey, Rupert and Jessica took the team one last time and escorted the team to their destiny. The next hour flew by and it was time to head toward the arena one last time. As the superstition dictated all of the parents followed the same routine as the first day. We all made our way to the seats closest to the ones we commandeered the day before. The blaring music and the flashing lights were all drowned out by the intense thoughts in my head, along with a prayer for the impossible. I have never wanted anything more for a team in my life. As proper cheer etiquette would dictate, we as parents should not ask for anything more than the team doing their best and representing their gym to the best of their ability. This time if we were to be honest with each other, we were selfishly all asking for a bit more this time.

The word was out that Peppermint made it to the finals and the venue was filled to capacity. People were stuck in the entrance of the venue as they would not allow anymore people in the arena. People were brimming with anticipation to watch all the teams including the Minnie Mints and Mickey. Our attention shifted to the staging area as the Red and White bows appeared from behind the curtain. The sea of the distinct blue and green uniforms cascaded into the staging area. The crowds shuffled once again as the final team before Peppermint completed their routine.

The bulk of the Stingray Nation descended upon the venue and the iconic pre routine chant started to erupt from behind the parents viewing area. " STINGRAYS! *Clap Clap* STINGRAYS! *CLAP CLAP* echoed throughout the arena. Peppermint heard the chanting and was bouncing in excitement. They began beaming with smiles as they knew it was about time to take the stage for the final time. The announcement was made and Peppermint stormed the stage to wave to all their adoring fans and parents. They each went through their pre routine rituals and took their positions. In unison they all locked eyes on the leader who has taken this team as far as they could possibly go. Their adoring eyes waited for the signal that would begin the last routine from this magical season. Once Coach Ashley was assured all were in the proper position. The final thumbs up hit the air and the music rang out one more time. WELCOME TO MINTLAND….. filled the arena and the team did exactly what they have done all year. With a near hypnotic precision Peppermint went through the entire routine just has the had hundreds of times before.

The Thumbs Up at Summit

As the routine pushed on, I could not help but play back the enitre season in my head as they continued to amaze on stage. I played back the struggles of learning the challenging "Stunt of Death," the injuries, the illnesses, the team bonding and friendships made, the successes, the failures, the frustrations, the dedication and sacrifice, the personal growth and maturity. The culmination of overcoming all of these challenges was now being awarded with this moment.

The spirit of this team was difficult to articulate to others, especially outside of the competitive cheer world. The epitome of what we as parents have been trying to explain to others all year was up on stage at this moment, the only problem was, I could not capture it in a bottle and share it with the people who were not here. The frustration of never properly explaining the full exuberance of All Star Cheerleading is why the network of people involved is such a tight knit group. No one can ever do justice or properly understand the explanation of why the sport is so magical, we just "get it".

When teams work, it's a chemistry that is built over time and culminates when everyone compliments and respects one another as a person, not just as an athlete. What was so incredible is that we were currently staring at this team who innocently and unknowingly bought into everything their coaches taught them. What we all admired about this team was the emanating innocence and loving spirit Peppermint carried in their hearts and inadvertently shared with everyone. You felt it everytime you were in their presence. They believed in themselves and each other and it was amazing to behold.

As my reflective journey came to an end, the roaring confidence emitting from the stage was evident. This team fought to prove they belonged every step of the way and their final performance would not be any different. With the emotions exuding from every facial expression and every count of their routine. The Minnie Mints and Mickey finished their last routine just as they have all year. With Beechers beaming smile and extended arms the last few seconds of Peppemints season closed with the final verse of the music. A few of the mints paused with hands extended in the air in the "praise hand" emoji pose. It was time to take in the moment, and they did just that. They all embraced and collectively left the stage for the final time. The crowd erupted in cheers as they hit zero once again. It was now out of the teams hands as they did everything they could dream of and more.

The coaches met up with Peppermint as they left the stage for the last time. The emotions of the moment were a lot to take in. The Coaches rang praise and thanked them whole heartedly for giving the best they could all year. The team dispersed and they scattered to find their families and friends. It would be only a few short minutes before the team had to reconvene for the final awards ceremony of the season.

Honestly, at that point it really did not matter where the team finished. The accomplishments of consistency and growth both athletically and personally were truly the main trophy for the year. The memories and legacy of this team would live longer than any reward. They rode the confidence and love for each other to places no one dreamt they could go. The teams all assembled on the stage as they always do.

The MC began to announce the team placements in reverse order. We knew that three teams hit zero on this day and possibly more. It was going to be close. The fifth and forth place team names were announced and the crowd cheered all of the teams as they made there way to receive team awards. It was down to the final three teams. We intently focused on the MC as he paused for a moment. He seemed to be focused on the sheet of paper in front of him as if to confirm what he was looking at before he spoke. He began to speak and he said the following, "Ok we will not have a third place finisher as we have a tie for second place." The crowd erupted in gasps. He started speaking again, "In second place The Stingray Allstars Peppermint!"and with that, It was over.

The amazing run of the Minnie Mints and Mickey resulted in a tie for 2nd place finish at Summit. We could not ask for anything more. We watched as the winning team was announced. We cheered the Champions on from Cheer Extreme, as they were truly amazing as well.

At that point, we all realized it was time to focus all of our efforts in comforting this team. You could only hope as a parent that they appreciated the moment, but we knew better. The most important thing we could do as parents is embrace the importance of this life lesson. The team immediately was escorted behind the stage to receive their medals and banner. We were instructed to meet the team around the side of the building. After what seemed like and eternity the door slowly opened and the team began to emerge. We were all trying to keep our emotions in check. We wanted to appear strong but as we suspected, the team came out and they appeared to be holding it together if only for the moment. Each of the children rushed into their parents arms.

Once I located my daughter she collapsed into my arms and cried. I wanted to make everything better. I wanted to explain the importance of what they accomplished to make her feel better. None of that was instantly going to take away the pain of coming so close to being a Summit Champion. It was going to take so time. The old fall back of Dippin Dots did not phase her. She wanted none of it.

I took her hand and we bagan the long walk across the football fields. About halfway across the large open field. I heard a faint yell behind me. " Mr. Eric ... Mr. Eric!" I turned around making sure the yelling was for me. Sure enough, off in the distance it was my buddy Beecher. He ran toward me and we turned to meet him halfway. As soon as we caught up with each other I noticed he had been a bit emotional as we all had. I wanted to break the ice, I said, "My goodness Beech I am so proud of you guys, you were so amazing" Beecher responded, "Thanks Mr. Eric, I just wanted to say thank you for helping us all year. You were a great team Dad."

At that point, I lost it. That simple statement of thanks he shared with me epitomized everything that we loved about this team. In his moment of sadness and need, Beecher took the time seek me out and thank me of all people. Overcome with emotion, I told him how incredibly proud of him I was, both as a Stingray and as a person. After we exchanged a few more words. I turned, grabbed my daughters hand and we finished the slow walk back to our cars. As we hit the main corridor, word had already spread about Peppermints second place finish. The amount of support and love we received by passers by was overwhelming. With each kind word my daughters spirits lightened just a little. After a cup of Dippin Dots and a few hours with teammates at the pool we were almost back to normal spirits.

The day after we returned from Summit my daughter was still a little disappointed in the result at Summit. I felt it was the appropriate time to share a story I had been thinking about over the past couple of months. As we always do, my daughter and I snuggle in bed and we talked about her 2nd place finish at Summit. I went on to explain the story that I felt she was prepared to hear, "The most treasured gifts one can receive in life are memories. Sometimes these are good memories, sometimes bad. While I know you were disappointed in not winning Summit, I want you to know this experience is a gift that you will be able to hold in her heart forever." She seemed a bit perplexed. I proceeded to tell her, "What your team accomplished will never be taken away. Your entire team will be able to take this experience with them for the rest of their life, and you can share the incredible journey with others, it is a gift. "Coach Ashley believing in you and giving Peppermint this incredible opportunity is something you should never forget. Peppermint overcame so many things to get as far as they did."

She seemed perplexed and responded, "What did we overcome? We were only doing our routine as we always do." I responded, "Honey, many people did not think you would do as well as you did. A few people thought that Peppermint was "too small" to compete in the Youth division. People said there was no way this team would be able to compete at UCA one time and get a bid; it was too much of a long shot. They should stay the course and go for the Triple Crown point race. A few people said they would never give a Mini team a "Youth Level" at large bid to the Summit. They were right, your team did NOT get an at Large bid, you were awarded a "Full Paid" bid instead. People were nervous when Peppermint changed the routine you guys worked on all season. It was a risky change going into Summit. It was a huge challenge and at times did not look so good in practice. A few people said maybe it was a mistake to change it. You hit it flawlessly both days in competition. People said there would be no way they would let a mini team move on to day two at the Summit in the Youth Division. You made it to day two final and finished in second place in the world in the youth division."

Kaitlyn then asked, "Why did our coaches not tell us all this stuff?" I responded, "Well sweetheart that is the gift that I was referring to. Coach Ashley, Kelsey, Jessica and Rupert believed in you so much. They knew you could do it all along without any doubt. That is the true gift! All of your coaches told you all year you were the best Mini Team in the world, and they were right. You get to hold that in your heart forever. The most important thing you can do with this gift is keep the spirit of this team and spread it in real life in everything you do. You can also share it with any future team you are on. Remember this moment, and share it with people in the future." With that I think she understood.

The following day I picked my children up from school. It was time for preparation for tryouts that started in four short days. We changed and headed up toward the gym. Upon arrival I looked around and there stood almost every single one of the Mini Mints and Mickey. As each one arrived, they all embraced, played, and began tumbling together. What they failed to realize was that in a few short days everything was going to be different. After tryouts the cycle of change would dictate the dawn of a new era for the Peppermints. Tryouts would take these children in many different directions and on many different teams and with new coaches in the coming days. I could only pray the miracle season of the Minnie Mints and Mickey live on in their hearts as they are truly "One of a kind." After they are placed with their new teams if I know them like I do, the passion and spirit will carry them forward "One more time."

The 2014-2015 Stingray AllStars Peppermint

Second Place at Summit

Eric J. Moran

ABOUT THE AUTHOR

Eric J Moran is an author that lives in Marietta, Georgia with his wife and two daughters. His day job is coaching sales teams at large media companies. His writing is inspired by youth sports and he is passionate about building winning teams and building unstoppable cultures. You can find him on Twitter @cRayCheerDad